Choosing Our Choices

Enduring Questions in American Political Life
Series Editor: Wilson Carey McWilliams, Rutgers University

This series explores the political, social, and cultural issues that originated during the founding of the American nation but are still heatedly debated today. Each book offers teachers and students a concise but comprehensive summary of the issues's evolution, along with the crucial documents spanning the range of American history. In addition, *Enduring Questions in American Political Life* provides insightful contemporary perspectives that illuminate the enduring relevance and future prospects of important issues on the American political landscape.

The Choice of the People? Debating the Electoral College
    by Judith A. Best, foreword by Thomas E. Cronin
A Wall of Separation? Debating the Public Role of Religion
    by Mary C. Segers and Ted G. Jelen, introduction by Clarke E.
    Cochran
A Republic of Parties? Debating the Two-Party System
    by Theodore J. Lowi and Joseph Romance, introduction by Gerald M.
    Pomper
Choosing Our Choices: Debating the Presidential Nominating Process
    by Robert E. DiClerico and James W. Davis

Choosing Our Choices

Debating the Presidential Nominating Process

Robert E. DiClerico
and
James W. Davis

ROWMAN & LITTLEFIELD PUBLISHERS, INC.
Lanham • Boulder • New York • Oxford

ROWMAN & LITTLEFIELD PUBLISHERS, INC.

Published in the United States of America
by Rowman & Littlefield Publishers, Inc.
4720 Boston Way, Lanham, Maryland 20706
http://www.rowmanlittlefield.com

12 Hid's Copse Road
Cumnor Hill, Oxford OX2 9JJ, England

British Library Cataloguing in Publication Information Available

Library of Congress Cataloging-in-Publication Data

DiClerico, Robert E.
    Choosing our choices : debating the presidential nominating process / Robert
E. DiClerico and James W. Davis.
        p.   cm. — (Enduring questions in American political life)
    Includes bibliographical references and index.
        ISBN 0-8476-9447-X (alk. paper) — ISBN 0-8476-9448-8 (pbk. : alk. paper)
        1. Presidents—United States—Nomination.   I. Davis, James W., 1920–
II. Title.   III. Series.
JK521.D49   2000
324.273'015—dc21   00-024863

Printed in the United States of America

♾ ™ The paper used in this publication meets the minimum requirements of
American National Standard for Information Sciences—Permanence of Paper for
Printed Library Materials, ANSI/NISO Z39.48–1992.

Contents

Foreword

Marc Landy

In the wake of the most expensive and one of the most tumultuous presidential nominating seasons in American history, it is appropriate to try to better understand that process and evaluate its merits. In this book Robert E. DiClerico and James W. Davis provide a clear and concise explanation of how the presidential nominating system operates and engage in an illuminating debate about its strengths and weaknesses.

No aspect of American political life has changed in modern times as radically as has the system by which Americans nominate candidates for president. As recently as the election of John F. Kennedy, the major role in candidate selection was reserved for city, state, and county party leaders who dominated their state's delegation to their party's national presidential nominating convention. Often, the actual choice of candidate was undecided prior to the convention. The choice occurred as the result of discussion and compromise among those leaders. Now the candidate is chosen as a result of party primaries which take place in four-fifths of all states. The candidate who wins the most primaries is then nominated. The party convention exists only to ratify that result. The power of the so-called bosses to choose the nominee has disappeared. The choice is made by the primary election voters.

Although the primaries occur within the rubric of a specific political party, they have come more and more to resemble general election contests. Because the candidates need to distinguish themselves from one another, they stress their mutual differences and call attention to each other's shortcomings as if they were partisan enemies. Because the only efficient means for sending their message to millions of voters in the various primary states is via television, the leading contenders spend tens of millions of dollars on political advertising.

Defenders and critics emphasize different elements of the current process. Defenders stress the virtues of openness and inclusiveness. In the old days only a very small number of people participated in the caucuses that chose convention delegates, and those participants were often subservient to the wishes of party leaders. Primaries invite the participation of ordinary voters. In many states it is not even necessary to be a registered member of a party to vote in its primary. Many millions of voters participate in the course of the presidential primary season. The primary system also encourages the participation of more, and more diverse, candidates. Candidates who are not in good standing with the party leadership may still decide to try their luck with the voters. Prior to the 2000 primary season, party leaders and the leaders of the most powerful constituency groups had by and large committed themselves on the Republican side to George W. Bush and on the Democratic side to Al Gore. The opportunity to take their case directly to the people enabled Bill Bradley and John McCain to strongly contest for the nominations and also permitted a whole raft of other candidates, including Alan Keyes, Steve Forbes and Gary Bauer, to make their distinctive voices heard.

Critics do not deny that greater openness and inclusiveness have been achieved, but they claim that it has come at the cost of a deterioration in the representative character of the choice process and in the quality of the nominees themselves. Although primaries increase participation, primary voting levels are usually still quite low when compared to those of the general election. And those who participate in primaries are very different in political outlook from ordinary voters. Republican primary voters are far more conservative and Democratic primary voters more liberal than the voter at large. Therefore the primary process is liable to polarize the choices available in the general election depriving the other voters of the more moderate alternatives they would prefer. Because party leaders are motivated more by the desire to win elections than by ideological purity, they are more likely than primary voters to choose electable candidates. They are also more politically knowledgeable in general and better informed about the virtues and foibles of the various contenders in particular. In the old days, party leaders were able to discuss matters and negotiate with one another in private; they could make good use of their knowledge to calmly and deliberately assess the alternatives and make a more reasoned and calculating choice. Therefore, critics contend, an undemocratic nominating process actually enabled a more democratic general election and resulted in the election of better presidents.

After providing a thorough and comprehensive analysis of the evolution of the nominating process from its beginnings two centuries ago, Davis and DiClerico ably present the case for and against the current system. A careful reading of their arguments provokes the reader to consider the impact of this particular political question on the very meaning and nature of the American democratic system. Because each argument appeals to different crucial political virtues—openness and inclusiveness versus representation and deliberation—readers are forcefully reminded that they can't have it all. To choose between different nominating options is really to choose between different visions of modern democracy.

The democratic vision underlying the present system is rooted in the Progressive movement of which Theodore Roosevelt was the most vivid and famous leader. It sought to remove the barriers separating the ordinary citizen from the levers of power. Through such vehicles as the presidential primary and the voter-initiated referendum it provided individual voters with a more direct say in candidate selection and in the formation of public policy. Not only would this new openness empower the voters, but by curbing the influence of corrupt and hidebound local leaders it was far more likely to entice the most broad-minded and talented people into politics and enable them to win the highest office.

The other vision is older. It is rooted in the concept of strong political parties originated by Andrew Jackson and Martin Van Buren. Its democratic understanding differed from that of the Progressives because it was less optimistic about how well voters fare when popular politics is conducted on a massive scale. It feared that demagogues would learn to manipulate the election process for their own corrupt and even tyrannical purposes. Although in principle the president was beholden to the voters, in the absence of a strong party structure he was not answerable to anyone in particular. Salvation lay in the creation and perpetuation of strong political parties at the local level. Because presidential aspirants would need the support of those local organizations to get elected and re-elected they would have to tame their own ambitions and accept party discipline. Party control of presidential nominations was the mechanism for creating meaningful presidential accountability. Tied to local leaders, the president would not be free to represent the people against them, but neither would he be free to mislead and manipulate the people in the absence of strong forces capable of calling him to task.

A good citizen learns how to choose. As this book shows, the most crucial choices at stake are not about picking one presidential candidate or the other but about how to structure the overall presidential selection process so that those political characteristics most essential to a democratic way of life are strengthened and maintained.

Part One

Debating the Presidential Nominating Process

1

Evolution of the Presidential Nominating Process

Robert E. DiClerico

The presidential selection process consists of two formal stages: the nomination of candidates in each party, followed by the general election. While both stages are important, the nominating process is arguably more crucial, for it determines the choices that are placed before us on election day. Noted student of politics E. E. Schattschneider speaks to this point in observing that "the definition of the alternatives is the supreme instrument of power."[1] Nor was it lost on William "Boss" Tweed, the notorious political boss of New York City's Tammany Hall, who astutely reminded his compatriots, "I don't care who does the electin', so long as I do the nominatin'."

In other democracies of the world, the "nominatin' " is done by party groups that range in inclusiveness from relatively small party executive councils (Germany), to party members in the national legislature (Australia), to a national party convention that in some ways resembles our own (Canada). But even the most inclusive of processes to be found in other countries fall well short of the role accorded the American citizenry in determining who their choices will be on election day. The participatory character that now defines the presidential nominating process did not exist from the beginning, however, but is the consequence of a lengthy evolutionary process. In this first chapter, we consider the major twists and turns that brought us to the current president-by-primary process.

CONGRESSIONAL CAUCUS

So admired was George Washington throughout the length and breadth of the country that his nomination for and election to the presidency was a

3

foregone conclusion. Such was not the case, however, for those who came after him. Following Washington's late announcement that he would not be running again in the 1796 election, there was not very much time left for prospective candidates to launch a campaign for the presidency. Accordingly, two competing factions within Congress, the Federalists and the Democratic-Republicans, used their newly created caucuses in that body to nominate a candidate. The Federalists chose Vice President John Adams as the presidential nominee and Thomas Pinckney as his running mate, while the Democratic-Republicans settled on Thomas Jefferson and running mate Aaron Burr.

More formalized by 1800, the congressional party caucus served as the nominating mechanism through 1820, with the members of each party in Congress meeting separately to vote on who would carry its banner in the general election. That the caucus failed to endure for longer than twenty years was attributable to several factors. For one thing, it came under heavy criticism from such notables as John Quincy Adams, Andrew Jackson, Henry Clay, and John C. Calhoun, all of whom were rejected for the Democratic-Republican nomination in 1824. Heavily burdened by factional disputes, and with more than half the members refusing even to attend its caucus, the Democratic-Republicans ended up choosing William C. Crawford for president. Adams, Jackson, Calhoun, and Clay, meanwhile, were put up for nomination by the legislatures in their respective states. Not only would Crawford go on to lose badly in the general election, but he finished behind Adams, Jackson, and Clay—an outcome reflecting poorly on the judgment of the caucus. A growing number of state and local party leaders also voiced their objections to the congressional caucus, arguing that it denied them any role whatsoever in selecting the nominee. Finally, the extremely limited number of participants in this process, derisively referred to as "King Caucus," seemed increasingly inappropriate as the mood of Jacksonian democracy began to take hold in the population[2]—a mood expressed only too clearly in a resolution passed by the Ohio state legislature in 1823: "The time is now arrived when the machinations of the *few* to dictate to the *many* . . . will be met . . . by a people jealous of their rights. The only unexceptional source from which the nomination can proceed is the people themselves; to them belongs the right of choosing."[3]

NATIONAL CONVENTIONS

Following a brief transition period during which presidential candidates were nominated by state legislatures or local conventions, the political parties adopted a new nominating mechanism—national conventions. First used in 1831, these conventions consisted of delegates chosen by each state's political party. The procedure for doing so varied. In some instances the governor chose the individuals who would make up his party's delegation to the national convention, while in others the party's state committee made the selection. The most common practice, however, was to have the delegates chosen by caucus-convention, a rather complicated process whereby party members caucused at the precinct or township level and selected delegates to go on to the county caucus, which in turn chose delegates to a state convention. This state-level gathering then picked a group of delegates to attend the party's national convention.

By the turn of the century many had become disillusioned with this method of nominating presidents as well. There was little opportunity for participation by the rank and file; it was perceived as being subject to near total manipulation by the party bosses; few regulations existed on convention procedures, and those were honored more in the breach; presiding officers at the conventions ruled with a heavy hand; strong-arm tactics were used to prevent some delegates from entering the convention floor, and to harass others once they got there; and many of the delegates chosen by the party organization proved to be unsavory characters more than willing to sell their votes to the highest bidder.[4] This state of affairs, along with other malfunctions in the political process, precipitated a reform movement by the Progressives that, among other things, sought to involve voters more directly in the nomination of presidential candidates. As a means of achieving this goal they called for the establishment of presidential primaries. Administered by the states rather than parties, primary elections enabled voters themselves to pick the individuals who would comprise their party's state delegation. In 1901, the Florida state legislature became the first to pass a statute permitting parties to choose their presidential nominee or delegates by primary. Four years later Wisconsin, birthplace of the Progressive movement, went even further by passing legislation requiring that all its delegates to the Republican and Democratic conventions be chosen by presidential primary. Choosing delegates, however, did not enable voters to register their preferences for presidential candidates themselves. Accordingly, in 1910, the citizens of Oregon decided to establish the first presidential "preference" primary in which voters were given an opportunity to express their preferences for a presidential candidate and then vote separately (on the same ballot) for the individuals they wanted as delegates. These delegates, moreover, were legally bound to vote for the presidential candidate who won the preference vote.[5]

The appeal of presidential primaries began to take hold and by 1916 some twenty-five states instituted primaries of one kind or another. The initial enthusiasm gradually waned, however, with only the state of Alabama adopting the primary method over the next thirty-two years, while eight others decided to abandon them. A combination of factors contributed to this change of heart: Party leaders exhibited little enthusiasm for them, the cost of running them was seen as high, turnout was low, and many presidential candidates declined to enter or campaign in them.[6] In subsequent years some states returned to the primary while others repealed it until "by 1968 the number appeared to have stabilized at sixteen states plus the District of Columbia."[7]

If the introduction of presidential primaries in the early 1900s did not wrest control of the nominating process from the party elites, nevertheless, in conjunction with other important developments, the primaries did gradually moderate elite influence over the next five decades. For one thing, primaries now provided concrete evidence of a candidate's popularity separate from and independent of the assessments made by party leaders. Public opinion polling, which began in the 1930s and thereafter grew steadily in significance, offered further external validation of a candidate's viability. To these factors we must also add advances in communication (radio and television) which enabled candidates to go over the heads of the party organization and communicate directly with voters, delegates, and even party leaders themselves. And we must add finally the willingness of candidates to establish their own campaign organizations separate from the party.[8]

All of these developments provided insurgent presidential candidates with leverage over the nominating process that would not have been possible otherwise. Thus, even though Senator Robert A. Taft (R-Oh.) was the Republican establishment's favorite for the nomination in 1952, Dwight Eisenhower's victory in the New Hampshire primary (even while still in Europe as NATO's supreme commander), along with the 100,000 write-in votes he received in Minnesota's primary, forced party leaders to sit up and take notice. His appeal was further confirmed by Gallup Poll trial heats showing him running stronger than Taft against all prospective Democratic rivals.[9] These indicators undoubtedly helped set the stage for what came next. At the Republican convention Eisenhower forces went before the Credentials Committee and boldly challenged a number of state delegations populated by Taft supporters, arguing that party leaders had dictated their preference to the delegates. Not surprisingly, the Credentials Committee, composed as it was of Taft loyalists, remained unmoved by such claims. Eisenhower supporters then took their fight to the convention floor and managed to win support for a "Fair Play" resolution which led to the replacement of the disputed Taft delegates and ultimately Eisenhower's nomination.[10] Of course, it certainly did not hurt that Ike was a war hero and as such popular with most party leaders, even if not necessarily their first choice.

The primaries also compelled party leaders to take seriously the presidential candidacy of Senator John Kennedy (D-Mass.) in 1960. Although he too was generally popular among the power brokers in his party, their enthusiasm was tempered by the fear that a Roman Catholic was simply not electable. Those fears were largely put to rest, however, following his victories in key primaries, including the heavily Protestant state of West Virginia. For those less popular among the party elites, however, primary victories or even favorable ratings in the Gallup Polls did not necessarily convert into victory. Senator Estes Kefauver (D-Ark.) ran for the Democratic presidential nomination in 1952 and lost despite leading in the polls and winning most of the primaries.[11] Nor, as we shall see shortly, did Senator Eugene McCarthy's (D-Minn.) strong showings in the Democratic primaries save him from a similar fate in 1968.

Senator Barry Goldwater (R-Ariz.), on the other hand, did manage to secure the Republican nomination in 1964 despite substantial opposition from national and state party leaders. Crucial to his success, however, was not his showing in the primaries, but the formation of a highly organized group of foot soldiers at the local level who infiltrated the caucuses in those states where the party organization was weak. Southern states in particular, where Republican party structure ranged from feeble to nonexistent, were prime targets of opportunity for Goldwater strategists.[12]

THE ERA OF REFORM, 1969–1988

As the 1968 election approached, Americans were growing increasingly frustrated by the Vietnam War. Our involvement in this Southeast Asian country had already imposed considerable social and economic costs upon the nation and yet showed no signs of moving toward a successful conclusion. For many rank-and-file Democrats, the frustration was all the greater because they appeared to have no alternative to the candidacy of Lyndon Johnson—a president who insisted that the United States stay the course in Vietnam. All at once Eugene McCarthy, a little-known Democratic senator from Minnesota, announced that he would seek the Democratic nomination as an antiwar candidate. In the first real test of his candidacy, McCarthy ran in the New Hampshire primary and succeeded in attracting 42.5 percent of the vote, while President Johnson finished with 49.5 percent. Despite the loss, McCarthy's showing was widely interpreted as victory, coming as he did within seven points of an incumbent president, and in a state known for its patriotic fervor. Sensing that Johnson was vulnerable, Senator Robert Kennedy (D.-N.Y.) threw his hat into the ring four days after the New Hampshire primary. As support for both grew, Johnson became convinced that his renomination was by no means a certainty. This assessment, combined with his desire to avoid having the war become a political football in the campaign, caused Johnson to withdraw from the race on March 31, 1968. Nearly one month later Vice President Hubert Humphrey, with the blessing and support of the White House, announced that he was entering the race. A campaign defined by surprises took yet another dramatic turn when Robert

Kennedy was assassinated just minutes after his triumphant win in the California primary. This left only McCarthy and Humphrey. At first blush, Mc-
Carthy would seem to have been in a strong position, since Humphrey had
entered the race late and did not run in a single primary. The reality proved
quite different, however, for by the time convention balloting was com-
pleted, Humphrey had swamped his opponent, winning 1,760 votes to Mc-
Carthy's 601. That the vice president won so decisively may be attributed to
two factors: first, a majority of the delegates in 1968, as in nearly every previous election in this century, were chosen not in primaries but rather by the
caucus-convention or appointment methods; second, both of these methods
were controlled by the party leaders, most of whom had aligned themselves
solidly behind Humphrey.

McCarthy and Kennedy supporters were both bitter and disillusioned by
how the nomination had played out in 1968. The Democratic national convention had in the final analysis chosen as its nominee an individual whose
views on Vietnam were not notably different from those of the President he
served. Moreover, in contrast to McCarthy and Kennedy, who took their
case to the people in the primaries, Humphrey had not entered a single primary contest. Further, during the nominating process McCarthy supporters
repeatedly found themselves victimized by arbitrary rules and procedures
used in connection with the selection of delegates. In fact, an informal group
calling itself the Commission on the Democratic Selection of Presidential
Nominees met for several weeks prior to the convention and catalogued the
structural and procedural drawbacks associated with the delegate selection
process. Their findings, which were presented to the Rules and Credentials
Committees and circulated among the delegates, prompted the proposal of
two resolutions which together required that state parties provide "all Democratic voters . . . a full, meaningful, and timely opportunity to participate in
the selection of delegates" to the 1972 convention.[13] Both resolutions passed,
although in light of the distracting protests outside the hall and the confusing
manner in which the resolutions were handled on the convention floor, it is
far from clear that delegates fully appreciated the implications of what they
had done.[14] The delegates also voted to establish a commission charged with
recommending ways to implement these resolutions.

McGovern–Fraser Commission (1969–1970)

Pursuant to the decisions made at the 1968 convention, the chairman of
the Democratic National Committee in 1969 constituted the Commission
on Party Structure and Delegate Selection under the chairmanship of Senator
George McGovern of South Dakota. (Congressman Donald Fraser of Minnesota assumed the chairmanship in 1971 when McGovern decided to seek
the presidential nomination.) We now consider the irregularities and defi-

ciencies in delegate selection identified by the McGovern–Fraser Commission, as well as the changes it proposed to correct them.

Party Rules

Participation in any game is nearly impossible if you do not know the rules about how it is played. To the astonishment of the commission, eight states had absolutely no rules covering the selection of delegates; in several others the rules were issued just prior to the start of the selection process; in still others, as we shall see shortly, rules existed, but they did not cover all aspects of delegate selection.[15] The commission therefore recommended that *all state parties adopt and make readily available rules on how delegates are to be chosen.*

Dates and Times of Meeting Places

Participation in the caucuses also requires that you know when and where they are going to be held. The commission found that party rules in some states were silent on this important procedural question, while in other states the rules authorized local party officials to determine the times and places of caucus meetings. In either case, party officials were left with the power to shape the outcome. In Louisville, Kentucky, for example, a local party leader held his precinct caucus outside in December so as to discourage participation. In neighboring Missouri, Democratic committeemen in four townships refused to disclose where and when their township caucuses would take place. McCarthy supporters managed to learn when one of these caucuses was to be held, only to discover that business was already well under way by the time they arrived. In another township a local party leader chartered a bus, loaded it with loyal followers and ample liquid refreshment, and held the caucus while travelling the interstate at sixty miles an hour.[16] The commission recommended that henceforth *the time and locations of all caucus meetings be published in advance. Further, the meetings in any given state must be held on uniform dates, at uniform times, and in places of easy access.*

Proxies and Quorums

During the course of their inquiry, commission members found major abuses of proxy voting, a procedure that permits one individual to vote in the name of one or more other individuals. In one township caucus, for example, McCarthy supporters were in the majority only to be outvoted when the presiding party official cast 492 proxy votes—three times the number of people present—for his own slate of delegates. At the state convention in Hawaii proxies were cast from a precinct which, following an urban renewal project, had been reduced mostly to vacant lots.

The commission's fact finding also revealed that quorum requirements for conducting party business were set too low. In Alabama, where the party state committee formulates new delegate selection rules every four years, only 23 percent of the committee had to be present in order to make this important decision. In Arizona, meanwhile, the state party committee was responsible for appointing the entire state delegation to the Democratic National Convention; yet it required a quorum of only 25 percent to conduct business.[17] The commission proposed that *proxy voting be abolished and that quorum requirements at party meetings be set at 40 percent.*

Unit Rule

Under this procedure the majority is able to bind the minority to vote for the majority's preference. Fifteen states using the caucus-convention method employed the unit rule at one or more stages (that is, precinct, county, or state convention) in the selection of delegates.[18] Believing that this practice prevented a fair reflection of voter preferences, the commission recommended that *the unit rule be abolished.*

Blind Primaries

In the states of West Virginia, Illinois, Pennsylvania, Florida, New Jersey, and New York, primary laws either prohibited or else did not require that individuals running for delegate express a presidential preference. Consequently, when voting for delegates voters had virtually no idea which presidential candidate a delegate favored. This arrangement contributed to an interesting anomaly in Pennsylvania which allowed voters to vote for delegates and then on another part of the ballot express their preference for a presidential candidate. Eugene McCarthy received 78.5 percent of the presidential preference vote and yet managed to win the support of only 24 of the state's 130 delegates.[19] For 1972, therefore, the commission recommended that *all delegates be given the opportunity to list their presidential preference on the ballot* (including the designation "uncommitted," if appropriate).

Untimely Selection

One of the more surprising deficiencies uncovered by the McGovern–Fraser Commission was the timing of the delegate selection process in some of the states. More precisely, twenty-four of the states had chosen all or a significant percentage of their delegates prior to the calendar year of the national convention. Thus, on the day that Eugene McCarthy declared his candidacy one-third of the national convention delegates had already been chosen. As the commission observed, "By the time the issues and candidates that characterized the politics of 1968 had clearly emerged, therefore, it was impossible for rank-and-file Democrats to influence the selection of these delegates."[20] To correct this problem the commission recommended that *all delegates be chosen during the calendar year of the convention.*

Appointment of Delegates

As already noted in this chapter, appointment constitutes one of the three methods by which delegates may be selected. The commission learned that in four states the *entire* delegation was chosen by the party's state committee; in another four states their party's committees were authorized to pick anywhere from a third to one-half of the delegates; and in two other states the governor alone had the power to appoint *all* of the state's delegation.[21] The commission saw these proportions as inappropriate in view of the fact that the appointment method does not allow for any input by the party rank and file. Accordingly, it proposed that in the future *no more than 10 percent of a state's delegation be chosen by the appointment method.*

Slatemaking

As the commission discovered, how individuals were nominated for delegate slots could have a decisive impact on those who were selected. In a number of primary states party officials put together "slates" of delegates who were automatically selected unless challenged on the primary ballot by another slate. Moreover, the party's delegate slate was identified as the "Party Endorsed Slate" on the ballot, and it was also given preferred ballot placement. Finally, the filing fee for a challenge slate could be quite steep in some states. In other primary states, meanwhile, challenging the party slate was simply not allowed. In states selecting delegates by the caucus-convention method, a number of party organizations failed to provide adequate notice of the party individuals responsible for drawing up delegate slates. The commission recommended that state parties *define the procedures by which slates are put together and challenged.*[22]

Ex Officio Delegates

Under this practice, state parties guarantee delegate slots to certain state party and public officials by virtue of the positions they hold. In states such as Washington, Maryland, and Colorado, for example, the percentage of delegate spaces reserved for these officials was 25, 27, and 14 percent, respectively.[23] Since voters have no opportunity to approve or disapprove of these officials, the commission recommended that *ex officio delegates be abolished.*

Discrimination

Regardless of how delegates were selected (i.e., caucus-convention, appointment, or primaries), the commission found that blacks, women, and the young were underrepresented at the 1968 Democratic National Convention. Although blacks constituted 11 percent of the population, with 85 percent of them having voted Democratic in 1968, only 5.5 percent of the delegates were black. As for women, they constituted 53 percent of the adult population and yet only 17 percent of the delegates were females. Delegates under the age of thirty held only 4 percent of the delegate slots. Having concluded that these data provided clear and convincing evidence of discrimination, the commission called for state parties to take *"affirmative steps to encourage representation . . . of minority groups, young people and women in reasonable relationship to their population in the state."*[24] Thus, for example, if 15 percent of the population of Illinois was black, then every effort must be expended to ensure that 15 percent of its delegates would be black as well; the same applied for women and individuals under the age of thirty. In those instances where a state delegation did not reach the required percentage, the burden of proof rested with the state party to demonstrate that it had made "a good faith effort" to comply with the rules on quotas. States that failed to demonstrate a good faith effort were subject to having all or part of their delegation replaced.

Costs, Fees, Assessments

The role of delegate to the Democratic National Convention could, as the commission discovered, carry with it a very substantial financial cost. In Connecticut, for example, the party's official slate of delegates gained free access to the primary ballot, while any challenge slate was forced to ante up more than $14,000 in filing fees. In Iowa and Indiana each state delegate was assessed $250.00 by the party, and Indiana slapped on an additional $250.00 charge to help defer the expenses for its hospitality suite at the convention. In addition to burdens such as these, delegates had to pay for their hotel accommodations and meals, expenses which in 1968 averaged $445.00. Given the costs incurred by delegates, it should not be surprising to learn that the income levels of delegates attending the 1968 convention were substantially above the population as a whole; 40 percent of the delegates made in excess of $20,000 a year, compared to only 12 percent of the population; 47 percent made between $10,000 and $20,000, in contrast with only 18 percent of the population; and finally, although only 13 percent of the delegates earned under $10,000 a year, fully 70 percent of the American people fell into this category.[25] Believing that the ability to serve as a delegate should not be unduly constrained by financial burdens, the commission recommended that *all costs and fees be limited to no more than $10.00. It also called upon states to find other ways to ease the financial burden of serving as a delegate.*

In 1972, the McGovern–Fraser Commission presented the above findings and recommendations to the Democratic National Committee, which accepted the report with only one exception, the National Committee's decision to allow its outgoing and incoming committee members to serve as ex officio delegates to the 1972 national convention.

Given that a number of the commission's recommendations served to significantly reduce the role of party leaders in the delegate selection process, some states predictably, but unsuccessfully, attempted to resist implementing them. By the time the 1972 convention opened, forty states and the District of Columbia had achieved full compliance, and the other ten were in substantial compliance. The latter ten's failure to reach full compliance was mostly due to the fact that legislative rather than party action was required to implement some commission recommendations. Seeking to explain why there was such a high level of compliance by the state parties, one student of the reform process concluded that "much of the credit must be given to the commission staff, a clever newspaper and publicity campaign designed to embarrass local parties into acting, the adroit maneuvering of the national chairman and his staff, and not to be forgotten, the goodwill and desire for improvement of hundreds of regulars and reformers who worked for change at the local levels of the party."[26]

Republican Party Reforms

The Republican National Convention in 1968 also authorized the creation of a reform group known as the Committee of Delegates and Organizations, which, among other things, was charged with inquiring into the delegate selection process. Unlike the Democrats, however, their recommendations did not take effect until 1976, since they had to be approved by the 1972 Republican convention. The committee's approved recommendations included a call for open meetings in the selection of delegates by caucus-convention; the development of information systems to make individuals aware of how they could participate in the selection of delegates; and a ban on proxy voting, ex officio delegates, and excessive fees. The committee also urged but did not insist that efforts be made to encourage the participation of blacks, women, young people, and senior citizens in the delegate selection process. Another Republican reform group (Rule 29 Committee) created after 1972 would echo this latter recommendation, but in the absence of any enforcement authority it had very little clout over state parties.

That the Republican party reforms proved considerably more modest than those of their Democratic counterparts is attributable to several factors. There was no constituency in the Republican party clamoring for reform. The party had, after all, captured the presidency in 1968 and would do so again in 1972 by a landslide. In addition, the leader of the party (Richard Nixon) was in the White House and saw little need to make sweeping changes in the process that helped put him there. Also, given the Republican party's long-standing philosophical commitment to "states rights" on matters of public policy, one would not expect its national party to dictate to the state parties on party matters. Finally, unlike the Democrats, Republican party reforms had to be approved by four separate bodies—National Committee Rules Committee, National Committee, Rules Committee of the national convention, and the national convention itself—the first three of which were dominated by party establishment types disinclined to institute major changes in the delegate selection process.[27]

Mikulski Commission (1972–1973)

The impact of the McGovern–Fraser Commission reforms was readily apparent as the Democrats convened in Chicago for their 1972 convention. Scarcely in evidence were members of Congress, big-city mayors, and other prominent state officials, all of whom had liberally populated previous conventions. On the other hand, among the delegates now present, 40 percent were women, 15 percent were black, and 22 percent were under thirty.[28] An outraged Richard Daley, mayor of Chicago and long one of the kingmakers in the Democratic party, stood by as fifty-nine of his Cook County delegates were removed from the convention hall for not complying with quota requirements and replaced with an alternate slate. Another power broker, the feisty AFL-CIO president, George Meany, was equally distraught over a quota system that had failed to include the backbone of the Democratic party—working men. The most dramatic impact of the reforms, however, was the nomination of the liberal insurgent candidate, Senator George McGovern (D-S. Dak.). The strong opposition by most of the party leadership alone would most likely have doomed his candidacy at previous conventions. This time, however, the increase in primaries, the opening up of the caucus-convention process, the ban on ex officio delegates, and the limit on appointed delegates all served to terminate the party leadership's control over the delegate selection process. But even though McGovern won the battle for the nomination, he was destined to lose the war. The party leaders, having played no role in his nomination, felt no obligation to work for him in the general election. Much of organized labor took the same position, refusing to endorse the Democratic party nominee for the first time in twenty years.

The controversy and ill feeling caused by the reforms moved the delegates to mandate another reform commission to reassess and refine the changes that had been made. Chaired by Baltimore City Council member Barbara Mikulski (now U.S. Senator for the state of Maryland), this group commenced its deliberations in April of 1973.

Only too aware of the hard feelings generated by the quota requirement, the commission recommended that it be jettisoned. In its place, the commission proposed that a state party be required to take "affirmative action"

toward including women, blacks, and young people in reasonable proportion to their numbers in the state's Democratic party. Furthermore, in determining whether a state party had in fact made a good faith effort to do so,
the burden of proof would now lie with the challenger instead of the party.

Responding to charges that the reforms had organized the party elites out
of the nominating process, the Mikulski Commission made two recommendations, both of which proved to be more cosmetic than real. First, Democratic governors, senators, and representatives were granted floor privileges
for the next convention. They could *not* vote, however. Second, whereas the
McGovern–Fraser Commission had restricted parties in primary states to
appointing no more than 10 percent of their delegates, the number would
now be raised to 25 percent. There was less to this increase than meets the
eye, however, for the Mikulski Commission stipulated that this 25 percent
must reflect the same distribution of candidate preferences as the delegates
chosen in the state's primary. This change had little success in bringing in
more public officials, most of whom did not necessarily want to be forced
to commit to a presidential candidate.

More consequential were the commission's efforts to ensure that voter
preferences would be more accurately reflected in the delegate selection
process. Toward this end, it proposed that the winner-take-all primary be
abolished—a proposal urged upon the states but not mandated by the Mc-
Govern–Fraser Commission. In this type of primary the candidate receiving
the largest share of the vote wins *all* of that state's delegates. In 1972, for
instance, Hubert Humphrey won 39.2 percent of the vote in the California
winner-take-all primary. His opponent, George McGovern, finished only
slightly ahead with 44.3 percent and yet walked off with all 174 of the state's
delegates. Arguing that this type of primary essentially disenfranchises all
those who vote for the losing candidate, the commission recommended that
henceforth all delegates be chosen in accordance with the *rule of proportionality;* that is, the percentage of delegates a candidate received would be proportionate to the percentage of the vote won in the primary. This rule was
also to be extended to the caucus-convention process. In order to qualify for
a proportional share of delegates in either the primaries or caucuses, however, a candidate had to reach a minimum support level of 10 percent. (The
Democratic National Committee would amend this proposal to 15 percent).
The commission, however, did permit one exception to the rule of proportionality: allowing a state to run a winner-take-all primary if its delegates
were chosen at the congressional district level rather than statewide. In 1976,
thirteen states, mostly large ones, took advantage of this "loophole" and ran
winner-take-all primaries.[29]

The commission sought to ensure a more accurate reflection of voter preferences in yet another way. It recommended that all individuals running as
delegates in either caucuses or primaries be required to designate which pres-

idential candidate they supported. Where state law prohibited such listings on the ballot, parties would be required to publicize in newspapers the names of those running as delegates, along with their presidential preference.

Finally, apart from abolishing the statewide winner-take-all primary, the only other major change proposed by the Mikulski Commission was to allow a presidential candidate to approve all individuals running for delegate under his name. The need for this change arose because some delegates, determined to attend the convention at any cost, allied themselves with the candidate they thought would win the primary rather than the one they really supported. Once safely at the convention, they dutifully cast their ballot for the candidate they officially supported, but then went on to support "the positions of other contenders (i.e., their real preference) on credential challenges or Platform or Rules Committee issues."[30]

To summarize, although the Mikulski Commission made some hand waves in the direction of the party leadership, these gestures were more symbolic than substantive. The major thrust of the recommendations was directed toward ensuring that the distribution of delegates at the national convention would reflect as accurately as possible the preferences of the voters. These recommendations were presented to the Democratic National Committee in 1974 and, apart from raising the proportionality threshold to 15 percent, were accepted largely as proposed.

Campaign Finance Reform (1974)

Nineteen seventy-four saw the adoption of another set of reforms as well. These reforms came from Congress, not the parties, and were directed at the financing of campaigns, rather than delegate selection. They were inspired by the Watergate scandals, some of which involved accepting and encouraging illegal campaign donations to the 1972 Nixon re-election campaign, often in return for political favors. While the legislation addressed disclosure requirements, contribution limits, spending limits, public financing, and enforcement, we shall consider here only those provisions that bear most directly on the nominating process.

Defining the nominating and general election stages as separate elections, Congress established contribution limits of $1,000 per election for individuals, and $5,000 for political action committees (PACs). The most innovative aspect of the finance reforms dealt with the funding of presidential nomination campaigns. Under the new law, presidential candidates for the first time in our history became eligible to receive *matching public funds* to help finance their run for the presidency. If they opt for those funds, however, they are then limited to spending no more than $50,000 of their own money for their nomination bid. To qualify for these public monies, an individual must first raise $5,000 in *each* of *twenty states,* in contributions of no more than

$250 dollars. The government then matches the first $250 dollars of any individual contribution (PAC money is not matchable). The total amount of matching funds, however, cannot exceed one-half of the total spending limit established for the nominating stage. This spending limit, adjusted for inflation every four years ($40 million for the 2000 nomination rate), *applies only to candidates who accept matching public funds.* In addition to this overall spending limit, the law also establishes state-by-state spending limits which, again, apply only to candidates accepting matching public funds. For example, in the 2000 nomination race those candidates will be able to spend no more than $1.13 million in Iowa and $661,000 in New Hampshire.[31] On the other hand, presidential candidates who decline matching public funds at the nominating stage are still subject to the contribution limits but are not bound by either the overall spending limit or state-by-state limits. In addition, they are also free to spend as much of their money as they wish. To date, only three presidential candidates have ever opted not to accept matching public funds—John Connally (1980), Steve Forbes (1996, 2000), and George W. Bush (2000). For these three, a personal fortune (Forbes), access to money from other sources (Connally), or both (Bush) enabled them to raise and spend more money than would have been possible under public financing.

Winograd Commission (1974–1978)

Given increasing concern over the proliferation of primaries, the Democratic National Committee in 1974 created a Commission on the Role and Future of Presidential Primaries. Without much debate, the 1976 Democratic National Convention decided to expand the jurisdiction of the group by redesignating it the Commission on Presidential Nominations and Party Structure. Responsible for fine-tuning the existing reforms and considering possible new ones, this commission began its work under very different political conditions from its two predecessors, for there was now a Democrat in the White House. As leader of his party, Jimmy Carter had considerable influence over the composition and recommendations of what came to be known as the Winograd Commission, after its chairman Morley Winograd, who also headed the Democratic party in Michigan.

In accordance with a decision already made by delegates at the 1976 convention, the commission eliminated the last vestige of the winner-take-all primary, notably the loophole provision that had allowed states to use this type of primary if they chose their delegates at the congressional district level.[32] The commission also decided to raise the threshold necessary to qualify for the proportional sharing of delegates, stipulating that in caucus states the bar could now be set at 20 percent and in primary states as high as 25 percent. This change was spearheaded by Carter stalwarts who wanted to reduce the risk of a challenge to his renomination in 1980.[33]

In the past, states typically set filing deadlines for primaries at thirty days prior to the date of the primary. Responding to pressures from the Carter members on the commission who wanted to impose a *mandatory* fifty-five-day filing deadline, the commission ultimately compromised and proposed that states be *permitted* to set them as early as ninety days. The president's allies no doubt fought for this change because they wanted to avoid a repeat of the 1976 race when Senator Frank Church (D-Idaho) and California Governor Jerry Brown entered the race late and defeated Carter in several of the May and June primaries.

The commission also required that henceforth all caucuses and primaries be closed to those voters who did not publicly declare their affiliation with the Democratic Party. In those instances where state laws prohibited "closed" primaries, a state party would have to switch to the caucus-convention method for choosing its delegates. The purpose behind this change was to put an end to the possible mischief making that could occur by allowing members of one party to vote in another party's primary.

Responding to criticism that the delegate selection process had grown too lengthy—twenty-one weeks in 1976—the Winograd Commission reduced it to thirteen weeks, beginning with the second Tuesday in March and ending with the second Tuesday in June. States would be permitted to hold their primaries and caucuses on any Tuesday falling within this window. The rationale for this change, however, was largely negated by the fact that Iowa, New Hampshire, Massachusetts, and Vermont were granted exemptions from the calendar. Thus, in 1980 Iowa held its caucus on January 21, New Hampshire scheduled its primary for February 26, and both Massachusetts and Vermont ran their primary contests on March 4.

Party leaders, scholars, and other political observers continued to complain about the lack of seasoned politicians present at the previous two national conventions. The commission tried to address this concern by proposing that each state delegation be expanded by 10 percent in order to provide slots exclusively for state party and elected officials. In states employing the primary, those officials were to be chosen by delegates who had been elected in that primary, while in the caucus states they were to be picked by delegates to the state convention. As party leaders saw it, however, this reform offered less than might appear at first. More specifically, they would not be able to attend the convention as free agents, for the commission stipulated that the 10-percent add-on must mirror the distribution of candidate preferences among the primary or caucus delegates in their state. Consequently, most party officials would ultimately decline to be included in the 10-percent add-on.[34]

In what would turn out to be its most controversial recommendation, the Winograd Commission took further steps to ensure that delegates reflected the presidential preferences of those who had voted for them. In 1976, twenty-two states already had "binding primaries"; that is, delegates who expressed a preference for a given presidential candidate were bound to vote for him/her on the first ballot. (In some states the binding requirement extended for more than one ballot, or until the candidate released them.) The commission now recommended that all primary and caucus delegates be bound on the first ballot. Not only that, but to protect against the possibility that a delegate might not remain loyal, the commission decided to give candidates the authority to replace any delegates who switched their votes to another candidate. Referred to as the "yank rule," this proposal also originated with the Carter camp, revealing the president's determination to leave no stone unturned in seeking to ensure his renomination.[35]

In June of 1978 the Democratic National Committee gave its blessing to the Winograd Commission recommendations but added a change of its own. Under pressure from female activists in the party, it required that at least half of the delegates to the 1980 national convention be women. This change won the full blessing of President Carter, who was eager to please a constituency critical of his lukewarm support of the Equal Rights Amendment and his strong opposition to federally funded abortions.[36]

Hunt Commission (1980–1982)

Jimmy Carter's failure to win re-election in 1980 only served to heighten calls for restoring the lost influence of the party elites in the nominating process. Had party leaders been given a greater say, it was argued, someone as inexperienced in the ways of Washington as Carter would never have been nominated in the first place. With this concern in mind, the Democrats set about creating yet another commission to consider, among other things, the role of the party leadership in the nominating process. Chaired by Governor James B. Hunt of North Carolina and officially designated the Commission on Presidential Nominations, its members decided the time had come to create a new category of delegates who could, if they chose, go to the national convention uncommitted to any candidate. Dubbed superdelegates by the media, these individuals would constitute 14 percent (568 delegates) of all the delegates (3,923) in attendance at the 1984 convention.[37] Included in this 14 percent would be up to three-fifths of the House and Senate membership, with the remainder consisting of state and local party and elected officials.

The nature of the 1980 nominating race prompted the commission to rethink the wisdom of abolishing winner-take-all primaries. Proportional primaries were seen as widening divisions within the party, as evidenced by the nomination battle between President Carter and his Democratic challenger, Senator Edward Kennedy (D-Mass.). Even though the senior senator from Massachusetts stood little chance of defeating Carter, the bitter struggle dragged on all the way to the convention, with Kennedy continuing to accumulate delegates in the proportional primaries. Had there been winner-take-all primaries, many felt his candidacy would have been dealt a decisive blow much earlier in the process. To prevent a debilitating campaign of this sort from happening again, the commission recommended that the winner-take-all primary be reinstituted in states choosing delegates at the congressional district level. In addition, states deciding to retain proportional primaries would be permitted to employ a "winner-take-more option" whereby the candidate receiving the most votes in a congressional district would be awarded a bonus delegate. Finally, as a further deterrent to narrow-based but potentially divisive candidacies, the Hunt Commission proposed that a candidate attain at least 20 percent support in a caucus or primary in order to qualify for delegates.

Delegates and political observers objected to the 1980 reform binding delegates to vote for their declared presidential preference on the first ballot, and found particularly demeaning the "yank rule" allowing a presidential candidate to replace any delegate judged to be disloyal. Critics argued that these rules served to rob convention delegates of any independent judgment on voting matters. Accordingly, the Hunt Commission urged that the "yank rule" be abolished, and in place of the first ballot binding requirement stated that "each delegate shall in good conscience reflect the sentiments of those who elected them."

The Hunt Commission continued to wrestle with the length of the primary/caucus season, deciding that 1984 contests would begin on March 13, with *no* states (i.e., Iowa and New Hampshire) being granted an exemption. The Democratic National Committee, however, responding to special pleas by Iowa and New Hampshire, caved in and allowed them to hold their contests earlier. The former would ultimately schedule its caucus for February 20 and the latter for February 28, thereby nullifying any attempt to shorten the length of the process.

Fowler Commission (1985–1986)

Following their unsuccessful runs for the presidency in 1984, both Jesse Jackson and Senator Gary Hart (D-Colo.) complained that their candidacies were unfairly disadvantaged by the rules. The bonus delegate rule and congressional district winner-take-all primaries, they argued, brought them decidedly fewer delegates than they deserved (together they had won 55 percent of the votes cast).[38] Furthermore, they charged that the qualifying threshold of 20 percent was set too high, as was the number of superdelegates, most of whom were hostile to "outsider" candidacies such as their own. Accordingly, in 1985 the Democratic National Committee created the Fairness Commission, which was charged with exploring these issues. Chaired by the former Democratic state chairman of South Carolina, Dan

Fowler, the commission members sought to accommodate some of the concerns voiced by the Hart and Jackson camps. The winner-take-all and bonus delegate options were eliminated, and the threshold requirement was lowered to 15 percent. The commission refused to budge, however, on the number of superdelegates. On the contrary, for the 1988 convention they recommended that the number of superdelegates be increased from 568 to 645 (15.5 percent), thereby enabling all members of the Democratic National Committee to attend the convention, along with all Democratic governors and 80 percent of the Democratic members of Congress.[39] The superdelegate total would be raised again to 772 (18 percent) for 1992 and to 850 (20 percent) for 1996.

Republican Reforms, 1973–1996

In the aftermath of the changes proposed by the Fowler Commission, the Democratic National Committee has not seen a pressing need to create any new commissions. Nor, it should be noted, did the Republican Party feel compelled to adopt any of the changes advanced by the post-1972 Democratic party commissions (i.e., Mikulski, Winograd, Hunt, and Fowler). Thus, in contrast to their counterparts in the Democratic party, the Republicans require no minimum threshold in order to qualify for delegates, leave it up to states to decide whether their primaries will be proportional or winner-take-all (approximately half use the latter), do not require a certain percentage of delegate slots for party and public officials, and, finally, do not mandate that 50 percent of the delegates be women.

The 1996 Republican National Convention did, however, make one substantive change in its delegate selection process for the 2000 nomination campaign. Alarmed at the growing number of states moving their primaries or caucuses to the front end of the process, thereby forcing candidates to campaign simultaneously in more and more states, the convention decided to award bonus delegates to states scheduling their contests later in the spring. Those holding off until March 15 were to have their delegations increased by 5 percent. The bonus grew to 7.5 percent for states that waited until April 15 and 10 percent for those that deferred until May 15 or later. This incentive plan was not exactly a resounding success, however, for California and Ohio decided to move their primaries up three weeks to March 7, and Michigan, Washington, and Virginia jumped from March into February.

A PARALLEL DEVELOPMENT: MORE PRIMARIES

Accompanying the wave of reforms that occurred between 1968 and 1988, especially within the Democratic party, was another highly significant development—the proliferation of primaries.

Although none of the commissions examined in this chapter either required or urged states to adopt primaries as a method for choosing delegates, nevertheless, a substantial number decided to do so after 1968. (See Table 1.1)

There are various explanations for this increase. Some states, it is argued, felt the complexities of the McGovern–Fraser Commission reforms (1969–1970) were such that they could be implemented more easily in a primary than in a caucus-convention system. It has also been suggested that party leaders saw the primaries as being less susceptible to capture by the McGovern forces than the caucus-convention process. The importance of these two explanations should not be overestimated, however, for primary legislation was pending in nine states before the McGovern–Fraser Commission was even called to order and in another four states by the time the 1971 reforms were ultimately approved. Moreover, the overall trend toward more primaries continued well after 1972. In all likelihood, some states, perceiving the broad-based sentiment for greater participation in the selection process, saw the primary as the most democratic method for selecting delegates. In other states the switch to primaries appears to have been motivated by a desire to provide favorite son candidates with an added boost. In 1976, for example, the Texas state legislature switched to the primary after its U. S. senator (Lloyd Bentsen) announced for the presidency. North Carolina did the same for its native (Terry Sanford), as did Georgia for Jimmy Carter.[40] Finally, and perhaps most important, state officials are well aware that primaries typically bring a state much greater media attention than caucuses and provide a substantially bigger boost to its economy, since candidates must expend substantially more money to run in a primary than a caucus. In this connection, a recent study found that the New Hampshire primary

Table 1.1. States Holding Presidential Primaries, 1968–2000

Year	Democratic Party	Republican Party
1968	15	15
1972	21	21
1976	27	30
1980	34	35
1984	30	30
1988	37	37
1992	40	39
1996	37	40
2000	44	43

Source: 1968–1996 taken from James W. Davis, *U.S. Presidential Primaries and the Caucus-Convention System: A Sourcebook* (Westport, Conn.: Greenwood Press, 1997), p. 14. Figures for 2000 taken from *Congressional Quarterly Weekly Report,* March 6, 1999, p. 568.

was responsible for bringing to that state some 1,500 temporary jobs and the purchase of goods and services totalling $210 million dollars. Twenty thousand mentions of the state in the media enabled it to promote itself at no cost.[41] New Hampshire, to be sure, is a special beneficiary of these spin-offs because of its strategic location in the primary process.

CONCLUSION

As we look at the development of the presidential nominating process in America, the contrast between what we started with and what we have could not be more stark. Initially, only one segment of the party leadership was involved in choosing its presidential nominee, with no involvement whatsoever by the rank and file. Thereafter, however, movement was steadily in the direction of making the process more inclusive. First, the sphere of participation was expanded to include all levels of the party structure, who assembled at a national convention to choose a nominee. With the introduction of primaries, more of the parties' rank and file began to have a say in the selection of convention delegates, even though the structure (e.g., blind primaries) and number of primaries at first limited that role rather significantly. With the dramatic changes that occurred in the 1970s—reforms of both the caucus and primary processes—and the concomitant increase in the number of primaries, the ability of the rank and file to determine the nomination outcome increased substantially. Thus, a process that began with complete control by the legislative party and no role for the citizenry has evolved into one in which the role of the party leaders is secondary to that of primary electorates—primary electorates who, in the presidential nominations of 2000, will be voting in forty of the fifty states.

Although few would advocate a return to the congressionally controlled nominating process, if only because it seriously compromises the principle of separation of powers, there is nevertheless great concern that the president-by-primary process has failed to strike a proper balance between the role of the party on the one hand and voters on the other, and that this failure has in turn had a number of unfortunate consequences for the way we choose our presidents. The next chapter addresses these concerns at length.

NOTES

1. E. E. Schattschneider, *The Semi-Sovereign People* (New York: Holt, Rinehart & Winston, 1960), p. 68.

2. Roy F. Nichols, *The Invention of American Political Parties* (New York: Free Press, 1967), pp. 262, 263; Austin Ranney, *Participation in American Presidential*

Nominations 1976 (Washington, D.C.: American Enterprise Institute, 1977), pp. 2, 3; James W. Davis, *U.S. Presidential Primaries and the Caucus-Convention System: A Sourcebook* (Westport, Conn.: Greenwood Press, 1997), pp. 9–11; Robert A. Dahl, "Myth of the Presidential Mandate," *Political Science Quarterly* 105 (Fall 1990), p. 367.

3. M. Ostgrogorski, *Democracy and the Party System in the United States* (New York: Macmillan, 1926). Quoted in Dahl, p. 367.

4. William Crotty, *Political Reform and the American Experiment* (New York: Thomas Y. Crowell, 1977), pp. 201, 202.

5. Davis, *U.S. Presidential Primaries and the Caucus-Convention System: A Sourcebook*, pp. 13–15.

6. James W. Davis, *Presidential Primaries: Road to the White House*, 1st ed. (New York: Thomas Y. Crowell, 1967), pp. 28, 29.

7. Ranney, *Participation in Presidential Nominations 1976*, p. 4.

8. John Haskell, *Fundamentally Flawed: Understanding and Reforming Presidential Primaries* (Lanham, Md.: Rowman & Littlefield Publishers, 1996), pp. 18–20.

9. Davis, *U.S. Presidential Primaries and the Caucus-Convention System*, p. 17.

10. Theodore Lowi, *The Personal President: Power Invested Promise Unfulfilled* (Ithaca: Cornell University Press, 1985), pp. 72, 73.

11. William Keech and Donald Matthews, *The Party's Choice* (Washington, D.C.: Brookings Institution, 1976), p. 185; George Gallup, *The Gallup Opinion Poll: Public Opinion, 1935–1971*, vol. 2 (New York: Random House, 1972), p. 1075.

12. Haskell, *Fundamentally Flawed*, pp. 18, 19.

13. *Mandate for Reform*, A Report of the Commission on Party Structure and Selection to the Democratic National Committee (Washington, D.C.: Democratic National Committee, 1970), p. 9.

14. Byron Shafer, *Quiet Revolution: The Struggle for the Democratic Party and the Shaping of Post-Reform Politics* (New York: Russell Sage Foundation, 1983), pp. 33–36.

15. William Crotty, *Decision for Democrats: Reforming the Party Structure* (Baltimore: Johns Hopkins University Press, 1978), p. 84.

16. Crotty, *Decision for Democrats*, p. 84; Kenneth Bode and Carol Casey, "Party Reform: Revisionism Revised," in Robert A. Goldwin, ed. *Political Parties in the Eighties* (Washington, D.C.: American Enterprise Institute, 1980), p. 7; *New York Times,* January 17, 1980, p. A26.

17. *Mandate for Reform*, pp. 23, 25.

18. *Ibid.,* p. 22.

19. Bode and Casey, "Party Reform: Revisionism Revised," p. 9.

20. *Mandate for Reform*, p. 30.

21. *Ibid.,* p. 19.

22. *Ibid.,* pp. 24, 35.

23. Crotty, *Decision for Democrats*, p. 94.

24. *Mandate for Reform*, pp. 26–28, 34; Crotty, *Decision for Democrats*, p. 77.

25. *Mandate for Reform*, pp. 30, 31; Crotty, *Decision for Democrats*, p. 81.

26. Crotty, *Decision for Democrats*, pp. 145, 133. See also Shafer, *Quiet Revolution*, part 2.

27. Donald Fraser, "Democratizing the Democratic Party," in Robert A. Goldwin, ed., *Political Parties in the Eighties* (Washington, D.C.: American Enterprise Institute, 1980), pp. 119, 120.

28. *Ibid.*

29. *Congressional Quarterly Weekly Report,* April 3, 1982, p. 751.

30. Crotty, *Decision for Democrats,* p. 229.

31. *New York Times,* July 16, 1999, p. A16.

32. The states of Illinois and West Virginia were exempted from this prohibition.

33. *Washington Post,* June 10, 1978, p. 2.

34. *Congressional Quarterly Weekly Report,* August 4, 1979, p. 1609.

35. *Congressional Quarterly Weekly Report,* December 26, 1981, p. 2563.

36. Warren Mitofsky and Martin Plissner, "The Making of the Delegates, 1968–1980," *Public Opinion* 3 (October/November, 1980), p. 43.

37. *Congressional Quarterly Weekly Report,* July 4, 1992, p. 19.

38. Davis, *U.S. Presidential Primaries and the Caucus-Convention System,* p. 27.

39. *Congressional Quarterly Weekly Report,* July 4, 1992, p. 19.

40. Bode and Casey, "Party Reform: Revisionism Revised," pp. 16, 17; James W. Ceaser, *Presidential Selection: Theory and Development* (Princeton, N.J.: Princeton University Press, 1979), p. 263; Ranney, *Participation in American Presidential Nominations,* 1976, pp. 6, 7.

41. *New York Times,* July 18, 1999, p. 12.

2

The Case against the Current Primary-Centered System

James W. Davis

The United States and France are the only two Western democracies that directly elect their presidents. In France the presidential candidates are nominated by a party congress, parliamentary coalitions, or by the candidates themselves (de Gaulle).[1] In the United States presidential candidates are selected by national convention delegates from all fifty states and several territories who have been selected by the voters in the presidential primary states or by party activists in the states using the party-sponsored caucus-convention system. Without doubt, the American presidential nominating system is the most complicated, convoluted, and protracted system in the Western world. The formal nominating campaign lasts more than six months, and the "invisible primary" campaign begins before the midterm congressional elections—two years before the presidential election. No wonder the typical American voter is sometimes confused about our presidential nominating system.

National conventions, it should be noted, have undergone a major transformation over the past three decades. Formerly, the national convention served as a forum where the various contenders battled for the nomination. The famous Eisenhower–Taft nomination fight at the 1952 GOP convention, for example, demonstrated how important the nominating function of conventions was in the pre-reform era.

In 1952 three-quarters of the delegates were selected in states using the caucus-convention system. Voters in state presidential primaries chose only one-quarter of the delegates. Many of these popularly elected delegates were not formally pledged to a specific candidate. Hence, these delegates were free to shift their choice from one candidate to another in search of a nominee with better prospects of winning the White House. But this system has changed drastically since the early 1970s. Adoption of the McGovern–Fraser reform rules in the Democratic party requiring formal delegate pledges, open caucuses, and no ex officio seats at the convention triggered the change. By 1984 the legislatures in over thirty-six states, including all ten of the most populous states, had adopted presidential primary laws in which the voters selected pledged delegates to the national convention. Since this legislation applied to both parties in most of those states, the Republicans, too, were swept along by this tide of reform.

TRANSFORMATION OF THE NOMINATING SYSTEM

With the shift to a primary-centered nominating system, the national conventions no longer remain deliberative bodies that assess the qualifications of the various candidates before settling on a single nominee. Instead, the national convention has become a "rubber stamp" for registering the decisions made in the primaries and caucuses long before the convention opens.[2] This new convention process has been likened to the ceremonial role of the Electoral College in presidential elections that merely reflects the outcome of the presidential vote in each of the fifty states.

As a result of the transformation in the nominating process, the decisive phase now takes place during the presidential primary season, not at the convention.

Strangely, the process of selecting presidential nominees has undergone a fundamental change over the past three decades even though the national nominating convention—the final decision-making body—has remained essentially unchanged. Why? The explanation is relatively simple. The proliferation of presidential primaries to more than three dozen states and imposition of mandatory delegate pledges by the parties or state legislatures has transformed the national convention from a deliberative body—a party conclave that formerly reached a decision on the nominee only by intense bargaining and multiballoting led by state party leaders—into a ratification assembly that automatically approves the "popular choice" of the presidential primaries as the party nominee.[3] Clearly, decision making at the national convention system has been replaced by a plebiscitarian primary-centered nominating system. Indeed since 1980, the winner of the primaries has become the de facto party nominee weeks before the convention opens.

With the preponderance of states now using presidential primaries, some party analysts are urging the adoption of a single national primary, in which the voters of all fifty states would cast their ballots for a party nominee on the same day. Critics, however, claim that a national primary would require a "run-off" primary because no candidate would likely receive a majority of votes in the first round; thus, it would be necessary to hold three national elections within one year to elect a president. They also argue that a national primary would be too expensive and favor nationally known candidates over less well-known contenders. Another set of critics, including one of the present authors, has urged that the parties move in the opposite direction by reducing the number of primaries and reinstalling the caucus-convention system in at least half the states of the union—a change that would bring more deliberation to the nominating process and enhance party building as well.

CRITICS OF THE CURRENT SYSTEM

National columnist David S. Broder, a staunch supporter of responsible political parties and their vital role in a democratic society, makes a strong case against the current system:

> In the present nominating system, the determinants of success are the size of the candidate's ambitions, the extent of his leisure time, and the tolerance of his family, his budget, and his job for almost unlimited travel.

> These characteristics have almost nothing to do with the qualities that make an effective president—as the results show. It is a recklessly haphazard way to choose the candidates for that demanding job.[4]

James L. Sundquist, a longtime Washington analyst, is equally critical of the existing system, which is likely, in his words, to produce the following type of nominee:

> He may be an outsider to the national political process. He may have no experience in the federal government he seeks to lead. He may be a neophyte in dealing with complex issues of foreign relations and the domestic economy. He may be in no sense the national leader of large and crucial elements of his own party.[5]

The presidential primary system lacks, Sundquist argues, the "peer review" that existed in yesteryear when members of Congress, state party leaders, and big-city bosses usually had a firsthand acquaintanceship, often spread over years, with the candidate selected by the national convention. They knew his strong points and his failings.

As Sundquist explains:

> There is no screening mechanism. A party nominee for president is someone who has been able to devote enough time to shaking hands in the early primary and caucus states and to forming an effective get-out-the-vote organization there, who has raised enough money to put himself on television throughout the primary season and who has proved to have popular appeal.[6]

The lack of candidate accountability to the party means that, if elected, he or she will have few ties to members of his or her party in Congress with whom he or she must work to win support for his or her agenda. Most likely, the candidate will have no network of experienced advisers to help avoid the political minefields of the nation's capital. Without strong political ties to his or her party, the nominee will lack a corps of public officeholders to come to his or her defense whenever he or she comes under criticism or suffers from the backlash of special interest groups.

Without close ties to his party organization, the primary-selected nominee, Sundquist warns,

> may be a stranger to the people in Congress with whom he has to work, and he may have little sense of how to get along with them. He may have little idea of the kind of talent he needs to help run the executive branch and no network of experienced advisers to help him find the way.[7]

Both commentators have warned their readers that the presidential primary system produces candidates who are good at campaigning but unskilled at governing. Some critics cite President Jimmy Carter as a prime example. Indeed, political scientist Thomas E. Patterson complains that

> the system encourages candidates to act on their own. They can assemble a personal staff, raise funds, and set up shop in Iowa and New Hampshire with the goal of gaining an early victory that will propel them into national prominence. If they are able to capture the news, they may be able to secure the nomination without even having to undergo peer review. The extreme case was Jimmy Carter who at the end of his campaign claimed that he was beholden to no one.[8]

Both major parties, it is generally agreed, should make it a top priority to select top-notch candidates who are not only effective campaigners but who also possess the qualities of character, judgment, experience, and the ability to work with other public officials. To be sure, no nominating system automatically guarantees that two good candidates will always be chosen. Conversely, no existing system will guarantee that two bad candidates will be chosen. But the nominating process should be constructed in such a way as to be directly related to the process of governing. Under the present primary-centered system there is nothing to require that the party nominee be in touch with U.S. senators, House of Representative members, and governors who all will share in the governing process. In the 1976 race, for example, several contenders—Senator Henry M. "Scoop" Jackson (D-Wash.), Senator Birch Bayh (D-Ind.), and Representative Morris Udall (D-Ariz.)—shared among them support from virtually all of the established groups within the Democratic party, its elected officials, and the national and state party leaders. Jimmy Carter, the winning nominee, had none of the party leaders' support throughout the nominating race. Still, he was able to move through the nominating process all the way to the White House as an anti-Washington candidate.

One of the main deficiencies of the current system has been cogently explained by one team of critics:

> The process of building the coalition needed to win the nomination is now completely separated from the process of building the quite different coalition needed to govern effectively. It requires very difficult organizing skills, it forces very different kinds of activities, and it even puts a premium on running "against the government."[9]

More than fifteen years ago, political scientist James W. Ceaser declared that the fundamental question for those seeking reform of the nominating process should be "whether to maintain the present system of direct democracy with its limited role for political parties, or whether to transform the system into a representative decision-making process under the auspices of political parties."[10]

Let's examine further the arguments against the current primary-centered system.

FRONT-LOADING OVERBURDENS
THE NOMINATING SYSTEM

In recent years the presidential primary system has been further complicated by the continued "front-loading" of the primary schedule, with more and more states shifting to the early weeks of the primary season. Front-loading has reached a crisis state. In the year 2000 the presidential primary schedule will find nearly 38 percent of all convention delegates being elected on March 7. Under the present schedule at least twenty-seven states will conduct primaries or caucuses and more than two-thirds of all delegates will be chosen before the end of March. Most likely, the nominee of both parties will be known by that date.

Front-loading favors the well-funded contender. With plenty of cash available, the well-financed candidate can hire a full-time staff and a corps of field organizers, and purchase a full schedule of television advertising in each state he or she is running in. Front-loading, on the other hand, creates a monumental problem for underfinanced candidates. Since three or more primaries may be scheduled on the same day—"Super Tuesday" in early March may have as many as ten primaries and caucuses scheduled on that day—the underfunded candidate is simply unable to mount an effective campaign in more than one or two states simultaneously.

Front-loading is anathema to outsider candidates who must depend upon one or two early-round victories in the primaries and caucuses to build "momentum" for campaigning in subsequent primaries. But if the nominating race is, in effect, telescoped into a three- or four-week period in March, the outsider candidate does not have sufficient time to capitalize on his or her momentum because most of the primaries and caucuses are bunched so close together.

Front-loading takes a nominating system that is already frenetic and tightly compressed and makes it even less deliberative. With this tightly compressed schedule, the voters in the primary states and party activists in the caucus states are not given sufficient time to digest and reassess, or possibly change their minds about, the strengths and weaknesses of each contender as new information becomes available. As Steve Forbes's campaign manager, Dal Col, has put it, front-loading benefits incumbents and career politicians because "it doesn't give the electorate a sufficient opportunity to contemplate, observe, and absorb the ideas that are presented by all the candidates but especially new candidates."[11]

A Republican task force, convened after the 1996 election, concluded that the front-loading process forced candidates to spend more time fund-raising and less time campaigning before the voters.[12] Thus far, front-loading has helped the front-runner clinch the nomination early. In 1996, for example, Senator Bob Dole's (R-Kan.) chief rivals in the Republican race—Steve Forbes, Pat Buchanan, and Lamar Alexander—matched him step-for-step in the first two weeks of the primary season, but then Dole's assets of name recognition, money, and state organizational support from governors in South Carolina, Michigan, Ohio, and Illinois overwhelmed his opponents. Dole locked up the GOP nomination before California voters went to the polls on March 26—the earliest that any candidate had ever clinched a contested nomination. As of this writing, it also appears that front-loading will enable George W. Bush, the clear leader in the polls, fund-raising, and party endorsements, to score an early knockout in the 2000 nomination race.

ABSENCE OF PEER REVIEW

Absence of "peer review" is, critics agree, a serious flaw in the current front-loaded presidential primary system. Nelson Polsby has described the process as follows:

> Peer review is a criterion which entails the mobilization within the party of the capacity to assess the qualities of candidates for a public office according to such dimensions as intelligence, sobriety of judgment, intellectual flexibility, ability to work well with others, willingness to learn from experience, detailed personal

knowledge of government and other personal characteristics which can best be revealed through personal acquaintance.[13]

Peer review does not automatically guarantee qualified candidates. The selection of Warren G. Harding by party leaders in a "smoke-filled room" at the 1920 Republican convention is proof enough of the fallibility of peer review. Nevertheless, the input from experienced party leaders on leading candidates can help weed out candidates who outwardly may appear to be attractive contenders but who lack good judgment and sound decision-making skills. This is not to say that peer review should be the sole method of selecting presidential candidates. But there should be minimal argument that "while as with any process, the alternative of providing no means for the assessment of potential Presidents by peers seems less desirable."[14]

Without the potentiality—or necessity—of peer review, Nelson Polsby warns, "the incentives for prospective candidates to maximize name recognition and minimal public service—would be overwhelming. If a presidential candidate dismisses peer review as inconsequential and chooses to place all of his chips on his ability to sway voters in the primaries, then the nominating process works at cross purposes with the process of governing which relies so heavily on accountability among elites."[15] Under these circumstances the absence of peer review is likely to lead to inferior government and popular disaffection with government by a substandard White House occupant. The cases of President Jimmy Carter and President Bill Clinton, who both avoided systematic peer review on their way to the White House are two recent examples of insufficient peer review.

Under the traditional mixed sytem, elected federal and state officeholders and party regulars had a major voice in selecting the nominee because they made up a majority of the national convention votes. Frequently, these party leaders knew personally the leading contenders—their strong points and their shortcomings. They were in a far better position to pick an experienced leader than the rank-and-file voters in the primary states, who had only limited knowledge of the strengths and weaknesses of the various candidates.

The absence of peer review has altered the campaign strategy of many presidential contenders—indeed, it affects the kind of candidates who enter the presidential sweepstakes. The current front-loaded presidential primary system favors the well-financed or celebrity candidate who can purchase a huge amount of television advertising to persuade voters that he or she is the most competent candidate in the nominating race. The current system opens the door to multimillionaire candidates whose chief qualification is their unlimited campaign treasury. The names of H. Ross Perot and publisher Malcolm S. "Steve" Forbes immediately come to mind. Although Mr. Perot, a self-nominated candidate of the United We Stand movement in 1992, did not have to run the presidential primary gauntlet, he spent over $60 million in the general election campaign, capturing 18 percent of the popular vote. In 1996, Steve Forbes spent over $34 million of his own funds in the primaries in his unsuccessful bid for the GOP nomination. He will very likely equal or exceed that amount in his 2000 bid for the presidency.

Without peer review, party nominations are wide open to be hijacked by any wealthy celebrity who wishes to make a run, no matter how limited his office-holding experience may be. Peer review by party leaders, on the other hand, means that the party leaders will have a greater opportunity to evaluate the various contenders, especially their decision-making ability and their willingness to work effectively with Congress.

Critics, however, of the Democratic National Committee's decision in 1982 to give national convention delegate seats automatically to a large bloc of uncommitted party leaders—dubbed "superdelegates"—viewed this move as "backsliding toward an elite-dominated system."[16]

Insider candidates, however, have found no objection to the superdelegate plan; indeed, they have been the chief beneficiaries of the new rule. Outsider candidates, on the other hand, have bitterly opposed the rule. In 1988, for example, Reverend Jesse Jackson complained loudly that although he won 18 percent of the vote in the primaries and caucuses, he received only 10 percent of the delegates and virtually no support from superdelegates. He argued that although superdelegates have not been in a position to broker a divided convention, they have had a significant impact on the delegate selection process, a factor that reinforces the front-runner's advantage.[17] In 1984, for example, almost all of the superdelegates supported former vice president Walter Mondale. Jackson proposed to decrease the number of PLEO (party leaders and elected officials) delegates by eliminating the automatic inclusion of members of the party's national committee. However, the Democratic National Committee in 1990 rejected the Jackson proposal.

PROPORTIONAL REPRESENTATION AND THE THRESHOLD RULE

Within the Democratic Party special rules—proportional representation and the threshold rule—have further complicated the presidential nominating process. The proportional representation rule has produced a number of unintended consequences for the national party, for its state affiliates, and for aspiring presidential contenders.

For the national party, proportional representation has sometimes extended the nominating campaign and has made it more difficult for the front-runner to obtain a clear majority of delegates. For the state party affiliates, proportional representation has diffused power and undermined the collective influence of party leaders and officials. For candidates, proportional representation has encouraged marginal candidates to focus on less competitive districts to pick up delegates, even with a poor showing, as long as their vote total exceeds the 15 percent threshold rule. Although proportional representation may assure broader representation and reflect rank-and-file sentiment more accurately, the cost to the party in failing to reach a consensus on the party nominee seems excessive.

Critics of the 15 percent threshold rule point out that the small percentage of votes needed to win delegates encourages multiple candidacies, factionalizes the party, and offers incentives to those without national experience, reputation, or even party ties to run. By winning the votes of as little as 15 percent of those participating in a primary or caucus, the politically-unknown candidate can win delegates, obtain recognition, and use this recognition to gain national standing in the nominating race.

CURRENT SYSTEM UNDERMINES COALITION BUILDING

Another major flaw of the current front-loaded primary-centered system is that it minimizes coalition building—the ultimate key to electoral success in November. Indeed, presidential candidates no longer follow the coalition-building route to win a majority of national convention delegates. As Thomas E. Patterson has put it, "Candidates have no great incentive to build links to their party leaders before the contest begins."[18] Instead, it's a case of "every man for himself" and "survival of the fittest." Without question, the new nominating system has fostered a candidate-centered system, in which each candidate establishes his or her own self-contained campaign organization, fully equipped with fund-raisers, pollsters, TV-time buyers, computer experts, press agents, and so on. The object is, of course, to capture a majority of national convention delegates at any cost. This means that candidates must mount an all-out attack on intraparty rivals, even though they will need the support of these rivals in the general election.

Nelson Polsby argues that the traditional mixed system, unlike the current plebiscitarian system, encouraged candidates to build ties with other leaders in the party. In the process the successful candidate would develop the skills and build party coalitions needed to pass legislation once in office.[19] A viable system requires, in John Aldrich's view, "a system that maintains the selection of credentiated candidates, that is, those who satisfy nominal demands of qualification; that encourages or assists candidates who are skilled in the art of persuasion among the other branches of government."[20] In Nelson Polsby's words, "Where parties are strong, coalition-building flourishes; where they are weak, the politics of factional rivalry prevails."[21]

Critics of the current system argue, as mentioned earlier, that it produces candidates who are far more skilled in the art of winning elections but who may lack the qualities of being an effective chief executive. Indeed, John Aldrich insists, "The need for public support induces a bias in the system that favors those who can best use the technology of public campaigning and who can invest the most and longest effort in campaigning."[22]

The post-1968 election reforms, it can be argued, focused on a single set of related problems—how to open up the delegate selection system and how to encourage greater public participation. But in the process they transformed the presidential nominating process into a popularity contest that rewards the candidate with the strongest and usually best financed campaign organization in a host of primary states. As John Aldrich has put it, "The consequence, partly intended and partly unintended, was rejection of the old coalition-building route and its complete supplanting with a mass popular campaign."[23] Clearly, the new nominating system affects the kind of candidates who benefit from the essentially plebiscitarian system who at the same time may lack the coalition-building skills and decision-making ability to govern the country.

DOMINANT PRESIDENT PRIMARY SYSTEM SPAWNS NEW TYPE OF CANDIDATE

The front-loaded primary-centered system, it seems more evident each succeeding four-year election cycle, attracts certain kinds of candidates to run for president—the super-ambitious contenders. Indeed, ambition is probably the highest motivating factor for presidential candidates in the age of television. To be sure, all presidential candidates must possess and demonstrate, at least indirectly, a high level of ambition. No candidate, it seems fair to say, can expect to reach the White House in the current era without unquenchable ambition. Consequently, campaigning ability has become the driving force in the nominating process, since there is no shortcut "to climbing the greasy pole," as Disraeli aptly described the leadership selection process in the nineteenth century. But the cost is high—perhaps too high. Erwin C. Hargrove, an authority on the presidency, has recently lamented that the current nominating processes for the president "are flawed in that they reward highly ambitious, even driven candidates who in the absence of peer review may carry their excesses into office."[24] Presidents Nixon, Carter, and Clinton, it can be reasonably argued, all fit this model.

Campaigning ability has also become an important factor in the march to the White House. Campaigning for high office, it seems clear, gives candidates a sense of how to sustain popular support. But crisscrossing the country for the better part of a year, especially during the primary season, is scarcely a good introduction to being president. The excessive length of the nominating campaign in the United States is virtually unknown in Western

Europe; election campaigns there rarely exceed thirty days. But the nominating system in our country imposes a high cost in turning potential presidential attention away from questions of effective government.[25]

In yesteryear less attention was focused on a candidate's public speaking and crowd-pleasing style. But in the current era, both ambition and campaigning ability are viewed as indispensable for a candidate wishing to be considered a serious contender.

Electioneering skills are, beyond question, a key factor under any nomination system. Even under the old mixed primary-caucus system, party leaders were reluctant to select a candidate deficient in these basic skills. But in the pretelevision age, campaigning skills were viewed as less essential. In the age of television, however, electioneering skills top the list of "availability" factors needed to win the nomination.

Unfortunately, electioneering skills are not synonymous with political leadership. Though it is relatively easy to recognize electioneering skills, it is less easy to identify in advance of the general election those elements that comprise effective governing skills. Successful electioneering does not necessarily reveal how a candidate will operate if he or she reaches the White House.

Near the top of the governing skills list would be the ability to deal with Congress, establish an agenda, and move bills into laws. Additionally, knowledge of the institutional workings of the federal government, the ability to command party loyalty for programmatic support, a talent for coalition building, ability to attract experienced staffers and cabinet members, and the ability to persuade the public at large to follow presidential leadership are all vitally important at 1600 Pennsylvania Avenue. Over and above these factors, a sound understanding of foreign policy and national security issues are also needed credentials.

This list of qualifications is a big order. The question then boils down to which type of presidential nominating system better serves the country and selects the best-qualified nominee: the traditional mixed-primary/caucus-convention system or the current system of presidential primaries, with its heavy overlay of plebiscitarianism.

LOSS OF SEQUENTIAL CYCLE

One of the chief shortcomings of the current front-loaded presidential primary nominating system is the loss of the sequential cycle of the traditional mixed nominating system. Until the vast proliferation of presidential primaries in the early 1970s, the mixed system operated at a rather leisurely pace so that party regulars (who usually become national convention delegates) could assess the leadership capabilities and political skills of the various contenders under a variety of electoral conditions over a four-month period from mid-February to mid-June. Furthermore, they had another month or so before convention time until they had to make a final choice of the party nominee at the national convention.

Under the old system New Hampshire did not hold the first-in-the-nation primary until circa March 10—town meeting day in the Granite State. Wisconsin, the second major test, did not conduct its primary until the first week of April—plenty of time for the candidates to shift their campaigns from New England to the Middle West. In the next four weeks only two more primaries were held. Thirteen of the seventeen presidential primaries were held in May or early June. Not until mid-May was more than one primary held on the same day. In 1968, for example, a majority of primary state delegates were not selected until late May.

John F. Kennedy's nominating campaign of 1960 is a classic model of the sequential process in operation. Kennedy also used the sequential cycle to confront a major religious issue. Until Kennedy's entry in the 1960 Democratic nominating race, the conventional wisdom was that no Roman Catholic could win the presidency, since it was alleged that he would be beholden to the Pope before deciding on major policy issues. New York governor Alfred E. Smith, the 1928 Democratic nominee, had been the only Roman Catholic nominee in the nation's history, and he was decisively defeated by Republican Herbert Hoover.

Kennedy opened his presidential bid with an easy victory in the New Hampshire primary. As a New England "favorite son," he had only token opposition. But he then moved his campaign to Wisconsin, an agricultural state, to confront his chief rival, Senator Hubert H. Humphrey of Minnesota, in a territory thought to be favorable to Humphrey. As a next-door neighbor, Humphrey had often been described as Wisconsin's "third senator." Kennedy, however, surprised the political experts and national media by defeating Humphrey in six out of ten congressional districts. Even so, some critics insisted that it was the heavy Catholic vote for co religionist Kennedy that provided the margin of victory in the Badger State. To answer his critics and demonstrate that his Wisconsin victory was not based on his religious affiliation, Kennedy decided to focus his campaign on the West Virginia primary, a state whose population was 93 percent Protestant. Kennedy's impressive victory—233,510 votes to 152,187 votes for Humphrey—convinced his critics and the big city Democratic mayors that Kennedy's Catholicism was not a handicap to winning the presidency. Kennedy's West Virginia victory knocked Humphrey out of the race and opened the road to the Democratic nomination.[26] Kennedy also won primaries in Maryland and Oregon as further proof of his "electability." No presidential candidate in American history has orchestrated the sequential nature of the primary system more effectively than John F. Kennedy.

By contrast, the current front-loaded primary schedule has completely overturned the sequential primary schedule. In 1996, for example, over twenty-five state primaries and caucuses were held in mid-March. Approximately 75 percent of all delegates were selected by March 26.[27] In the year 2000 it is expected that nearly 70 percent of all delegates will be chosen in a two-week period between March 7 and March 20. Under the front-loaded system a vast majority of delegates will be forced to make a choice for presidential nominee more than four months before convention time. Clearly, the last vestiges of the sequential review process of potential presidential nominees have disappeared. If national conditions change, or if some damaging new information on the de facto nominee surfaces, the pledged delegates will be locked into their choice and unable to shift to a more acceptable candidate.

DISPROPORTIONATE INFLUENCE OF IOWA CAUCUSES AND NEW HAMPSHIRE PRIMARY

The current front-loaded presidential primary centered system fails to distribute power more evenly across the electorate. Voters in the first caucuses in Iowa, and the first-in-the-nation New Hampshire primary, exert a disproportionate influence—indeed almost decisive influence—in the presidential nominating process. Although Iowa's Democrats in 1976 chose only 47 out of 3,008 delegates (1.5 percent) to the national convention, Jimmy Carter's victory in the caucuses catapulted him from obscurity to front-runner status overnight. In 1976, James I. Lengle has pointed out, "Jimmy Carter was transformed from dark horse to nominee by appealing initially to only 34,000 voters (11,000 in Iowa and 23,000 in New Hampshire)—or fewer people in two states combined than currently live in Hilo, Hawaii."[28]

As one team of researchers has noted, "Iowa is not typical of the nation. It does not have large urban centers, it has a small minority population, its culture and economy are more heavily dependent on agriculture than many states, it has a lower than average crime, and higher than average literary rates."[29] The state has a higher percentage of senior citizens. It has lower rates of unemployment. Iowa exceeds the national mean in the percentage of the population who have graduated from high school and in per capita newspaper circulation.[30]

New Hampshire, with a population of slightly over 1 million, constitutes less than one-half of one percent of the nation's population. It has no huge metropolitan centers and no large bloc of Hispanic or black voters. The New Hampshire national convention delegation rarely exceeds 25 members out of more than 4,000 at the Democratic convention and less than 20 out of 3,000 at the GOP conclaves. Yet the Granite State exerts more influence over the presidential nominating strategy than any single state, with the possible exception of California. Almost half of all the media coverage in the 1976 nominating race was devoted to the New Hampshire primary. According to Michael Robinson, "In proportionate terms, each Democratic vote [in 1976] in New Hampshire received 170 times as much network news time as each Democratic vote in New York. Media reality—television reality—implied that a victory in New Hampshire totally overwhelmed a victory in New York."[31] The media coverage given to the Iowa caucuses now rivals that of the New Hampshire primary. In their saturation coverage of these two states, the media are not concerned about which candidate might be more representative of his party or better for the country. Instead, the media are far more interested in winners and losers than with the basic issues facing the country. Significantly, of the twenty-eight Democratic or Republican candidates who entered the Iowa caucuses or the New Hampshire primary between 1972 and 1988 and who finished third or worse in both states, twenty-four were eliminated as candidates shortly thereafter.[32] In 1996 Texas Senator Phil Gramm bowed out of the presidential race after he finished fifth in the Iowa caucuses. Within three weeks of the New Hampshire primary, all of Senator Bob Dole's GOP rivals, except commentator Pat Buchanan, had withdrawn from the Republican nominating race. Clearly, no two states in the Union wield more power in the presidential nominating sweepstakes than Iowa and New Hampshire. No wonder critics find serious flaws in the current presidential nominating system.

LOSS OF THE SECOND-CHOICE OPTION

In a crowded field of candidates the division of the primary vote is likely to be fragmented, with the winner collecting only 30 percent or so of the vote. But this low figure often represents a first-place finish, and in a state such as Iowa or New Hampshire, a first-place finish will generate a huge amount of national media coverage on the television networks and cover stories in the weekly news magazines. The fact remains, however, that 70 percent of the electorate preferred other candidates. Nelson Polsby has put it this way: "The rule of thumb for candidates is, it is far better to be the first choice of 30 percent of the delegates in a non-deliberative system than the second choice of 90 percent."[33]

Jimmy Carter in 1976 was the first nominee in the post-reform era to master the mathematics of first-place finishes in a crowded field. In the 1976 Iowa caucuses, for example, Carter won first place—actually the uncommitted delegates exceeded Carter's total by 10 percent, but the national media conveniently ignored this fact. As a result, Carter skyrocketed into the headlines overnight. With this huge lift-off he then moved over to New Hampshire to face another crowded field. Once again, Carter outpaced the seven-candidate field to win first place with 28.4 percent of the vote, nosing out second-place finisher Morris Udall, who won 22.7 percent of the vote. Carter also benefitted from the fateful decision of his chief rival, Senator Harry M. "Scoop" Jackson of Washington, to skip the New Hampshire primary in order to concentrate on the Massachusetts primary. Jackson's decision cost him dearly. With two straight first-place victories in a row, Carter catapulted into the lead of the Democratic nominating race—a lead that he never relinquished. In New Hampshire only 5,000 votes separated Carter from second-place finisher Morris Udall, who split the Democratic liberal vote with three other liberal Democrats. But Carter walked off with all the laurels and Udall became just another "also ran." Overall, Jimmy Carter won seventeen primaries in 1976, but he collected only 39 percent of the primary vote.[34] In other words, over 60 percent of the presidential primary voters preferred candidates other than Carter. However, to place second under the current system is to finish out of the money, even though the second-place finisher might be more experienced and possess superior coalition-building skills. No wonder Nelson Polsby has cautioned "that the mass persuasion system that has effectively replaced party elites as the mechanism for selecting presidential nominees, especially in the Democratic party, comes with a significant price attached."[35] Under the old system party professionals, through deliberation and bargaining, could choose a candidate who, though perhaps not the front-runner in the polls and primaries, was nevertheless most qualified and most acceptable to major elements in the party. In the presidential primary-centered system, however, there are no mechanisms to consider second or third choices. As Wilson Carey McWilliams has put it, "The primaries have small place for second choices, even though like second thoughts such selections are more likely to reflect a concern for the good of the whole."[36]

CENTRALITY OF THE MASS MEDIA IN THE PRESIDENTIAL NOMINATING PROCESS

The emergence of television as the foremost communications medium of the twentieth century has had a negative impact on the caucus-convention nominating system. Political scientist Richard L. Rubin has explained how television and presidential primaries have been made for each other:

> Rather than initiating renewed interest in primaries, the prime political role of television . . . was in legitimating the primary process as the genuinely democratic way to choose convention delegates. The basic political posture of television journalism toward alternative nominating processes was to favor primaries versus state caucuses-convention methods, both in amount of coverage and the

positive nature of the story treatment. . . . The positive treatment of the primaries as a process was in part due to the fact that television, compared to print
journalism, had (and still has) far more difficulty in covering stories of complex
elite negotiations (such as occur in caucuses and state conventions) than election
campaigns and action-oriented events.[37]

Television network executives find the excitement of presidential primary
competition irresistible. Who is ahead in New Hampshire? How will the
candidates do on "Super Tuesday?" What do the polls reveal about the public's rating of the various candidates? The TV networks thrive on these questions, whereas local precinct meetings are unexciting, and the results are not
always easy to discern. In a presidential primary state the networks, operat-
ing out of their special studios in the state capital, can usually pinpoint the
winner before midnight, a few hours after the polls close. In some caucus
states, the results may not be known for a week or ten days because local
precinct officers are slow in forwarding their results to the state party head-
quarters. Since the networks are interested in fast-breaking news and do not
wish to spend money to monitor precinct caucus results across the state, the
caucuses receive limited coverage.

As the television networks focused more attention on presidential primaries in the 1960s and 1970s, some observers noted a direct correlation between the rise of television and the proliferation of primaries. Richard L.
Rubin, for example, indicates that in the early 1980s television played a major
role in tipping the balance toward the continued spread of presidential primaries.[38]

Against this media pressure to give heavy coverage to presidential primaries, the caucus-convention system has barely managed to survive in a
dozen states.

Over the past quarter century the primary-centered system of presidential
nominations has been hijacked by the mass media. With the rapid proliferation of presidential primaries and the recent front-loading of the campaign
schedule, the mass media have assumed a major—some say a decisive—role
in the presidential nominating process. In the early stages of the race the
media are the first to assess the prospects of the various unannounced contenders. By the time of the off-year, midterm elections the mass media have
begun rating the chances of the various aspirants. In the early fall of 1998,
for example, the Cable News Network hired the Gallup Poll to begin conducting "trial heats" between two potential contenders in the year 2000 election—Vice President Al Gore for the Democrats and Texas governor George
W. Bush, the leading GOP contender. These early polls showed that Bush
held a nearly 20-percent lead over Gore. Also, the same poll showed that
most of Bush's GOP intraparty rivals except Elizabeth Dole had failed to
rise above single-digit support. With most of the public still indifferent to

the politics of nomination, the mass media occupy a central role as chief evaluator or "handicapper" of presidential candidates in the early stages almost by default.

The mass media have utilized several criteria for assessing the various contenders—their public track record, the candidates' ratings in the opinion polls, and the ability to raise campaign funds. Unless a candidate rates fairly well in all three categories, the mass media will either ignore the candidate entirely or dismiss the low-rated contender to the marginal category. Former North Carolina governor Terry Sanford, a contender in the 1976 Democratic race, learned early in the race that the ability to raise money had suddenly become a major criterion—at least in the eyes of the national press—for measuring the viability of a presidential candidate. Sanford discovered that members of the national press refused to take his candidacy seriously until he met the twenty-state matching fund requirement of the 1974 Federal Election Campaign Act. Sanford's staff and those of several other candidates were told specifically by some media representatives in midsummer 1975, according to one source, that they would not be given coverage for the 1976 race until they qualified for federal matching funds.[39] Several campaign managers complained to reporters, and Mr. Sanford objected publicly to viewing subsidy qualification as a "license to practice."[40] Nevertheless, the national press largely ignored Sanford and the other candidates until they qualified for Uncle Sam's matching dollars. At this juncture, there does not seem to be much doubt that the ability to raise the necessary matching money will become a national media benchmark for measuring the candidates' credentials.

The press, according to Thomas E. Patterson, determines "electability" by focusing attention heavily on the candidate who it believes has a chance of gaining the nomination.[41] Unlike the general election, voters in the presidential primaries are not anchored by party loyalties and most are relatively uninformed about the various candidates and their positions on the major issues. The press, Patterson argues, is not routinely motivated by considerations of which candidate might be more representative of his or her party or better for the country.[42] Indeed, the mass media are not seriously concerned about the purpose the nominating process was designed to serve.[43] Instead, the mass media are driven primarily by news values, which attach paramount importance to picking the winner. Moreover, the mass media give a highly selective account of the events unfolding in the nominating process. And as Thomas Patterson observes, "The press treats issues as tokens in a strategic game and prefers issues that are lively and controversial."[44] As the late V. O. Key noted more than three decades ago, the news media "fail by far to meet the standards of performance, cohesiveness, and respectability that characterize the political party."[45]

Nor do the mass media have the ability to organize the choice facing voters in the presidential primary states. In Thomas E. Patterson's words, "The media while playing an important role in the campaign are not designed to serve as a political broker."[46] Consequently, the media cannot be expected to perform satisfactorily as the political intermediary between the candidates and the public.

By expanding presidential primaries in two dozen new states between 1972 and 1984, state lawmakers, in effect, handed over to the mass media several major functions formerly performed by political parties: establishing standards of performance for the candidates, designating the leading contenders, evaluating prospective winners in a multicandidate race, and setting the agenda for the contenders. Unfortunately, the mass media cannot serve as a satisfactory intermediary between the candidates and the rank-and-file voters because the media are far more concerned about the "horse race" aspects of the race, not the qualification of the various candidates or the basic issues of policy and leadership. No wonder Thomas Patterson complains: "By emphasizing the game dimension of the day the press forces it to the forefront, strengthening the voters' mistrust and reducing their sense of involvement. The press has this effect because the game schema drives its analysis and its capacity to see the campaign in other ways."[47] Above all, the media produce two commodities "all candidates want, namely, name recognition and momentum."[48]

That the mass media are not eminently suited to serve as the intermediary between the public and the candidates in the presidential nominating process may be disputed, but columnist Walter Lippman, more than seventy-five years ago, explained why the media do not provide a reliable basis for judgment.[49] News, according to Lippman, is found in events rather than in the underlying forces shaping society. Thomas E. Patterson, a keen admirer of Lippman, has pointed out that the mass media now operate under the pressure of a twenty-four-hour news cycle and deadlines. The constant pressure to meet deadlines and "scoop" the opposition leaves little time for evaluation and viewing events in context. In Patterson's words, "The press is necessarily guided by its own conventions and organizational imperatives, and these are certain to dominate its decisions. Consequently, the media cannot be expected to organize political choice in a coherent way."[50]

Nevertheless, the mass media have not been shy in arrogating to themselves a variety of functions that directly affect the process. First of all, the mass media have displaced the party in "winnowing out" the weak candidates in the race. Indeed, weeding out the weak candidates over the years has been a brutal business, and the mass media have operated with surgical efficiency. In the 1980 GOP nominating race, for example, the mass media, in effect, consigned at least four GOP candidates to the sidelines: former Texas governor John Connally, Senators Bob Dole and Howard Baker, and Representative Philip Crane. In the 1988 Democratic presidential race the mass media winnowed out several candidates. Former Florida governor Reubin Askew and South Carolina senator Ernest "Fritz" Hollings were quickly tabbed "also rans"; both dropped out less than a week after the New Hampshire primary. Also, the mass media quickly dismiss candidates who run out of campaign funds. Though the financially strapped candidates may be reluctant to face reality, the media do not hesitate to write them off in short order. No doubt Lamar Alexander's withdrawal from the 2000 race—six months before the first primary—was heavily influenced by media reports that his financially strapped campaign was now doomed following a poor showing in the August straw poll in Iowa.

Another major role performed by the press is what researchers call "priming," which is "the capacity of the press to isolate particular issues, events, or themselves in the news as criteria for evaluating politicians."[51] As Michael W. Traugott has described the process, "The priming concept is a variation of 'agenda-setting' and explains how issues shift in importance to an audience as cues provided by the media change."[52] Research indicates that when the news focuses on the governmental performance of a candidate, voters tend to judge the candidate on this criterion. If, on the other hand, the press "primes" the news by focusing on the private behavior of a candidate, many voters will judge the candidate on just that.[53] As a result, the mass media frequently set the agenda for the voters that will affect their voting patterns on primary day. The concept of priming goes beyond agenda setting, however; it suggests that the "play" of the story on television will affect not only the dimension of presidential evaluation but the valence (whether he is evaluated positively or negatively) of it as well. In short, the effect of "priming" leaves the candidates largely at the mercy of the media. Returning to the old mixed system would help neutralize the powerful role of the mass media.

Failure to reach double digits in the opinion polls early in the presidential election year is usually a tip-off by the mass media that the candidate cannot be considered a serious contender. Single-digit poll ratings mean that the news media will relegate those candidates to the "also ran" category.

TRADE-OFFS IN NOMINATING SYSTEMS

Evaluation of any presidential nominating system involves trade-offs. Indeed, as Scott Keeter and Cliff Zukin have pointed out, "any nominating system will promote certain values at the expense of others."[54] The current system, above all else, prizes "openness." However, a system that maximizes openness will most likely minimize experience and party ties. Thus, any system that fosters openness will give outsider candidates an easier opportunity to run and thereby give the electorate in the primary states a wider field of candidates from which to choose. But the cost may be high: electing nominees who lack experience and the organizational ties needed to govern effectively.

Good decision making on presidential nominations puts value on the properties of deliberation and reconsideration. The traditional mixed system usually left all options open for delegates on the choice of presidential candidates right up to the balloting at the national convention. With most national conventions unhampered by iron-clad delegate pledges, they could reserve judgment on candidate choice to the final hours or minutes before the roll call vote began.

Under the traditional system late-shifting developments abroad, unanticipated political turmoil in the nation's capital, or a smoldering scandal might dictate a shift in a candidate choice. But under the current mandatory primary system, national convention delegates are locked into voting for the candidate they have pledged to support in the primaries. In other words, the current system lacks the flexibility and resilience needed to adjust to rapidly shifting political conditions. In some presidential election campaigns the lack of flexibility may not matter. But in 1940 the fall of France to Hitler's conquering troops, for example, forced a rapid shift from isolation within the Republican ranks to a more internationalist posture and increased support for Great Britain. Reluctantly, many Republicans were forced to recognize that "Fortress America" was no longer a viable doctrine in the face of Hitler's threatened domination of Europe and the Middle East.

Similarly, in the late spring of 1996 some Republicans began having second thoughts about de facto nominee Senator Bob Dole serving as the party standard bearer. Dole was seventy-three years old and he had failed to offer a coherent campaign plan of attack on President Clinton and the Democrats. But so many delegates were pledged to him that it would have been virtually impossible to switch to another prospective nominee. Nor was there a charismatic candidate, such as Wendell L. Willkie in 1940, standing in the wings awaiting the call from the convention.

For purposes of comparison, the 1940 scenario deserves a brief review. New York governor Thomas E. Dewey led the Republican field by a considerable margin, with 360 votes out of a total of 1,000 delegates on the first ballot. Senator Robert Taft of Ohio had 189 and Wendell L. Willkie had 105 votes. Senator Arthur H. Vandenberg of Michigan, another isolationist, had 76, and Governor Arthur James of Pennsylvania had 70, with a scattering of votes among the favorite sons.[55] The field began to narrow on the third ballot. Dewey continued to lead, but his total dropped to 315. Willkie jumped into second place with 259 votes, and Taft followed in third place with 212 votes. On the fourth ballot, Willkie moved into the lead with 306 votes, Taft followed with 254 votes, and Dewey dropped to third place with 250 votes. At the end of the fifth ballot the race narrowed to Willkie, an avowed internationalist, with 429 votes and Taft, a leading isolationist, with 377, but none of the other contenders held enough votes to switch and give Willkie a majority. Willkie, however, went over the top on the sixth ballot, after the Michigan delegation switched from Vandenberg to Willkie and other state delegations followed suit, giving him a clear majority with 655 votes.[56] This brief recapitulation of the old-fashioned mixed primary/caucus system illustrates how much flexibility the old system possessed and how rigid is the current front-loaded presidential primary system. Generally, the de facto nominee is known well in advance of the convention. In yesteryear state party leaders and their delegations decided on the presidential nominee. Today the voters in the primaries select the nominee.

Under the current primary system voters select pledged delegates who have no choice but to follow their marching orders at the national convention. Delegates now serve merely as "messengers" or instructed delegates for the voters in the primary states. They have no voting latitude, especially if an international crisis develops, an economic recession suddenly hits, or a personal scandal involving the prospective nominee begins to circulate in political circles.

Of course, leadership problems of a president who has won his way to the top via the primaries cannot be attributed exclusively to the wide open nominating system. The Madisonian separation-of-powers system virtually guarantees that the president will experience difficulties bridging the gap between the executive and legislative branches whenever questions of public policy are involved. But a presidential selection process that shunts political parties aside in favor of a plebiscitarian process that rewards televised popular appeals without reliance on a political party as an intermediary may produce popular leaders who lack the vision and experience required to guide the country. All the great and near-great presidents of the United States have been strong party leaders—Thomas Jefferson, Andrew Jackson, Abraham Lincoln, Theodore Roosevelt, Woodrow Wilson, and Franklin D. Roosevelt—who did not reach high office merely by catering to popular whim or the latest opinion poll results.[57]

Formerly, the president could rely on his party to blunt the incessant demands of special interest groups that flourish in the nation's capital. But in a primary-centered nominating system presidential candidates largely ignore party ties to concentrate on winning popular support. As a result, if they reach the White House, new presidents cannot count on the party members in Congress to push their agendas and keep the special interest groups at arm's length.

Some critics of the primary-centered system are willing to state for the record that the public alone may not be the best judge of the qualities needed to become president. According to political scientist Austin Ranney, "The absence of peer review means that the candidates are chosen by people who know them only as faces on television and as personalities described by the news media; they are not chosen by people who know them personally and who have worked with them in situations of stress that show a person's true leadership qualities. Candidates are strangers, not peers reviewed by peers."[58]

NOTES

1. James W. Davis, *Leadership Selection in the Six Western Democracies* (Westport, Conn.: Greenwood Press, 1998), pp. 129–156.

2. James W. Davis, *National Conventions in an Age of Party Reform* (Westport, Conn.: Greenwood Press, 1983), pp. 245–282.

3. Byron E. Shafer, *Bifurcated Politics: Evolution and Reform in the National Party Convention* (Cambridge, Mass.: Harvard University Press, 1988).

4. David S. Broder, "Endless Primaries Net Endless Candidacy," *Washington Post,* June 5, 1980, p. 5, as quoted in *Presidential Primaries and Nominations,* William Crotty and John S. Jackson III (Washington, D.C.: CQ Press, 1985), p. 64.

5. James L. Sundquist, "The Crisis of Competence in Our National Government," *Political Science Quarterly* 95 (Summer 1980), p. 193.

6. *Ibid.*

7. *Ibid.*

8. Thomas E. Patterson, *Out of Order* (New York: Random House, 1994), p. 216.

9. Jeanne J. Kirkpatrick, Michael J. Malbin, Thomas E. Mann, Howard R. Penniman, and Austin Ranney, *The Presidential Nominating Race: Can It Be Improved?* (Washington, D.C.: American Enterprise Institute, 1980), p. 14.

10. James W. Ceaser, *Reforming the Reforms: A Critical Analysis of the Presidential Selection Process* (Cambridge, Mass.: Ballinger, 1982), p. 179.

11. Quoted in Larry J. Sabato, *Toward the Millennium: The Elections in 1996* (Boston: Allyn & Unwin, 1997), p. 59.

12. Larry J. Sabato, *Toward the Millennium,* p. 170.

13. Nelson W. Polsby, *Consequences of Party Reform* (New York: Oxford University Press, 1983), p. 170.

14. *Ibid.*

15. *Ibid.,* p. 171.

16. William Crotty and John S. Jackson III, *Presidential Primaries and Nominations,* p. 35.

17. Stephen J. Wayne, *The Road to the White House: The Politics of Presidential Elections* (New York: St. Martin's Press, 1996), p. 99.

18. Thomas E. Patterson, *Out of Order,* p. 218.

19. Nelson W. Polsby, *Consequences of Party Reform,* pp. 64–71.

20. John Aldrich, "Methods and Actors: The Relationship of Processes to Candidates," in *Presidential Selection,* eds. Alexander Heard and Michael Nelson (Durham, NC: Duke University Press, 1987), p. 184.

21. Nelson W. Polsby, *The Consequences of Party Reform,* p. 66.

22. John Aldrich, "Methods and Actors," p. 184.

23. *Ibid.*

24. Erwin C. Hargrove, "The Study of Political Leadership: Bill Clinton as a Test Case," in *PRG Report,* newsletter of the Presidency Research Group of the American Political Science Association, vol. 21 no. 2, Fall 1998 (Washington, D.C.: American Political Science Association, 1998), p. 14.

25. Richard Rose, "Learning to Govern or Learning to Campaign," in *Presidential Selection,* p. 71.

26. Theodore H. White, *The Making of a President* (New York: Atheneum, 1961), pp. 1–179.

27. William A. Mayer, *In Pursuit of the White House 2000: How We Choose Our Presidential Nominees* (New York: Chatham House, 2000), p. 23.

28. James I. Lengle, "Reforming the Presidential Nominating Process," in *Quest for National Office,* eds. Stephen J. Wayne and Clyde Wilcox (New York: St. Martin's Press, 1992), p. 306.

29. Walter J. Stone, Alan I. Abramowitz, and Ronald B. Rappaport, "How Representative Are the Iowa Caucuses?" in *The Iowa Caucuses and the Presidential Nominating Process,* ed. Peverill Squire (Boulder, Colo.: Westview Press, 1989), p. 21.

30. Peverill Squire, "Iowa and the Nominating Process," in *The Iowa Caucuses and the Presidential Nomination Process,* p. 8.

31. Michael J. Robinson, "TV's Newest Program: The Presidential Nominations Game," *Public Opinion* (May–June, 1978), pp. 41–46.

32. Peverill Squire, "Iowa and the Nominating Process," p. 10.

33. Nelson W. Polsby, "The News Media as an Alternative to Party in the Presidential Selection Process," in *Political Parties in the Eighties,* ed. Robert A. Goldwin (Washington, D.C.: American Enterprise Institute, 1980), p. 62.

34. James W. Davis, *Presidential Primaries: Road to the White House,* 2nd ed. (New York: Thomas Y. Crowell, 1967), p. 98.

35. Nelson W. Polsby, "The News Media as an Alternative to Party in the United States," in *Political Parties in the Eighties,* p. 64.

36. Wilson Carey McWilliams, "The Meaning of the Election," in *The Election of 1988,* ed. Gerald M. Pomper (Chatham, N.J.: Chatham House Publishers, 1989), p. 173.

37. Richard L. Rubin, *Press, Party and Presidency* (New York: W. W. Norton, 1981), p. 192.

38. *Ibid.,* pp. 192–193.

39. F. Christopher Arterton, "Campaign Organizations Confront the Media Environment," in *Race for the Presidency,* ed. James David Barber (Englewood Cliffs, N.J.: Prentice-Hall, 1978), pp. 14–15.

40. *New York Times,* July 13, 1975.

41. Thomas E. Patterson, *Out of Order,* p. 188. The discussion in this section relies heavily on Patterson.

42. *Ibid.,* p. 191.

43. *Ibid.*

44. *Ibid.,* p. 192.

45. V. O. Key Jr., *Southern Politics* (New York: Knopf, 1949), p. 16.

46. Thomas E. Patterson, *Out of Order,* p. 206.

47. *Ibid.*

48. William Schneider, "The Rapporteur's Summary," in *Before the Nomination: Our Primary Problems,* ed. George Grassmuck (Washington, D.C.: American Enterprise Institute, 1985), p. 128.

49. Walter Lippman, *Public Opinion* (New York: Free Press, 1965; reprint).

50. Thomas E. Patterson, *Out of Order,* p. 209.

51. Stephen Ansolabehere, Roy Behr, and Shanto Iyengar, *The Media Game* (New York: Macmillan, 1992), p. 148.

52. Michael W. Traugott, "The Media and the Nominating Process," in *Before the Nomination: Our Primary Problems,* p. 111.

53. Shanto Iyengar and Donald R. Kinder, *News That Matters* (Chicago: University of Chicago Press, 1989), p. 5.

54. Scott Keeter and Cliff Zukin, *Uninformed Choice: The Failure of the New Nominating System* (New York: Praeger, 1983), p. 187.

55. Richard C. Bain and Judith H. Parris, *Convention Decision and Voting Records,* 2nd ed. (Washington, D.C.: Brookings Institution, 1973), p. 255.

56. *Ibid.*

57. James W. Davis, *The President as Party Leader* (Westport, Conn.: Praeger, 1992), p. 1.

58. Austin Ranney, Testimony before the Senate Committee on Rules and Administration, as quoted by James W. Ceaser, *Reforming the Reforms,* p. 96.

3

In Defense of the Presidential Nominating Process

Robert E. DiClerico

Perhaps no feature of the American political process has been subject to more sustained and searing criticism over the last thirty years than the way we go about selecting the presidential nominees of each political party. From scholars, journalists, and public officials alike has come the charge that there is a great deal wrong with the presidential nominating process. The distinguished democratic theorist Robert Dahl regretfully concludes that "a sensible method of nominating presidential candidates still seems beyond the reach of Americans."[1] The dean of American political journalists (David Broder) finds the process to be a "wrecklessly haphazard way to choose the candidates for that demanding office."[2] And the late Terry Sanford, one time governor, U.S. Senator (D-NC), and presidential candidate, opined that "we expect to pick our president . . . by participatory disorder that knows no equal in American society."[3]

One can reject general indictments of this nature and still acknowledge that the current president-by-primary process has drawbacks—as does any method of selection. The most glaring of these is the much-discussed problem of "front-loading," a phenomenon characterized by primaries and caucuses bunching up at the front end of the contest schedule. This trend has been occurring gradually over the last several elections, becoming particularly pronounced in the 1996 and 2000 nomination races. But if front-loading is a serious problem, it is also relatively easy to solve, provided political parties have the determination to do so. Parties, after all, have the authority to organize the primary/caucus calendar and can levy heavy penalties on states that fail to comply. The Democratic Party has in fact threatened to do so in the past but ultimately acquieseced to the special pleadings registered by certain states.[4]

One may also question the influence that Iowa and New Hampshire exert over the nominating process. Unlike front-loading, however, which has virtually no redeeming features, the Iowa/New Hampshire problem is not quite so clear-cut. Admittedly, neither state is demographically representative of the nation as a whole. New Hampshire, particularly, has only 0.4 percent of the population, few urban areas, low union membership, and scarcely any blacks or Hispanics within its borders. On the other hand, because of these states' relatively small size, candidates of limited funds can compete effectively against more moneyed opponents, and voters have an opportunity to observe candidates "up close and personal." New Hampshire voters, moreover, appear to be more knowledgeable about politics than the nation as a whole, are attentive to the campaign, learn from it, and are not greatly swayed by the media's horse-race-type coverage.[5] New Hampshire natives would no doubt also add that their primary has had an impressive record of picking the next president—1992 being the notable exception, when Bill Clinton finished second with 24.7 percent of the vote.

Iowa and New Hampshire enjoy the influence they do because the former is the first caucus, and the latter the first primary. Facing no competing contests on the same day, they capture all of the media attention. Like front-loading, the disproportionate influence of Iowa and New Hampshire is essentially a calendar problem and could be quickly resolved if each party decided that it would no longer allow these two states, or any other, to hold their contests outside the window established for scheduling primaries and caucuses.

The critics of the nominating process, however, see many more problems than those just noted. Indeed, their complaints surfaced well before front-loading became a serious problem. In the following pages, I will argue that the critics have undervalued the strengths of the president-by-primary process, while often overstating the benefits of the system it has replaced.

MORE PARTICIPANTS

In 1996, some 22.5 million Americans participated in the presidential nominating contests held throughout the United States and its territories.[6] Under the old system (i.e., pre-1972), where most delegates were chosen by the caucus-convention method instead of primaries, participation in the nominating process was extremely limited. Even with the opening up of the caucuses in the aftermath of the McGovern–Fraser Commission reforms (1971), participation in primaries continued to far outdistance those turning out for the caucuses. For example, Austin Ranney found that participation in the twenty-one caucuses in 1976 averaged 1.9 percent of the voting population in a given state, while primary participation was ten times higher at 19 percent.[7] Or consider the difference in participation rates of states that have switched from caucuses to primaries. After 1972, one of the major switches came between 1984 and 1988, with seven states deciding to abandon the caucus system for primaries. Table 3.1 shows the seven states that switched in the Democratic Party, along with the participation rate for each state under both systems. The total number of individuals voting in these seven Democratic primaries in 1988 (4,178,180) is 7.5 times greater than the total number of participants in the seven Democratic caucuses held in these same states four years earlier. Thus, if one is seeking to make the nominating process more inclusive, the primaries appear to be decidedly more effective in this regard than caucuses.

Some critics, however, have suggested that a greater number of participants does not necessarily mean greater democracy. As Newton Minow put it:

> Presidential primaries were designed to take the nomination away from the party bosses in the back room and to give the decisions to the voters. But they haven't worked out that way. Instead, the current version of primaries turns the decisions over to a new kind of boss. Today, a small, unrepresentative handful of party activists, often concerned only with one issue or with narrow, special interests, dominate the primaries. Because the broad center of moderate and independent voters seldom vote in the primaries, the decisions are abdicated to small groups of motivated extremists of the left or right.[8]

Table 3.1. Democratic Party Caucus and Primary Participation in Seven States, 1984 and 1988

State	Democratic Party	
	1984 Caucus	1988 Primary
Arizona	34,173	497,544
Kentucky	16,000	318,721
Michigan	132,000	212,668
Minnesota	66,000	100,000
Mississippi	20,000	361,811
Missouri	40,000	527,805
Oklahoma	42,800	392,727
Texas	200,000	1,766,904
TOTAL	550,973	4,178,180

Source: Data compiled from Gary Orren, "The Nomination Process: Vicissitudes of Candidate Selection," in *The Elections of 1984,* ed. Michael Nelson (Washington, D.C.: Congressional Quarterly Press, 1985), p. 38; Gerald Pomper, "The Presidential Nominations," in *The Election of 1988: Reports and Interpretations,* Gerald M. Pomper (Chatham, N.J.: Chatham House, 1989), p. 40.

It is, of course, true that primary turnout is not impressive, ranging anywhere from 31 to 36 percent, depending upon the election year. Moreover, primary voters are typically older, more educated, more well-off, and more interested in politics than the population as a whole. This profile is scarcely surprising, however, for such individuals have always been overrepresented in elections at all levels and in other forms of political participation as well. The crucial question is whether primary voters also evince an ideological orientation that is unrepresentative of their party rank and file in general. Although there is some evidence to suggest that this might have been the case in the Democratic primaries in 1972,[9] other, more extensive inquiries have found little trace of it. A study of the 1972, 1976, and 1980 elections conducted by the Center for Political Studies at the University of Michigan found no significant differences between primary voters and party identifiers in primary states; nor, for that matter between a party's primary voters and its rank and file nationally. Moreover, in 1976 and 1980, the ideology of rank-and-file members "matched most closely with that of primary voters who supported the party's front runner."[10] Subsequent studies have persuasively argued that in seeking to measure the potential distorting effect of primary voters, it is more appropriate to compare them to those who voted in the general election but *not* the primary. The results of these investigations once again reveal few significant ideological differences between the two groups.[11]

Deeply troubled by the proliferation of primaries, some have called for their total elimination, replacing them with caucuses, while others seek a better balance between the number of primaries and caucuses.[12] This view grows out of their conviction that caucuses allow for more careful deliberation than primaries, and nurture party building as well. No doubt the latter is true, as is the extended opportunity that caucus-goers have to deliberate with each other. Whether the results of those deliberations reflect the views of the rank and file as accurately as the primaries, however, is open to very serious question. Indeed, for people such as Newton Minow (quoted above) who are worried about ideological extremists and single-issue enthusiasts distorting the process, that fear is more likely to be realized in caucuses than primaries. Caucuses by their very nature are likely to attract more ideological and intensely committed individuals, for caucus-goers are required to surrender an entire evening and publicly reveal a presidential preference or lack thereof. Primary voters, on the other hand, need only go to the polls and spend a few moments pulling a lever or marking a ballot.

Let us not forget that the most conservative and ideologically driven candidate to be nominated in this century, Senator Barry Goldwater of Arizona, failed to win a single contested primary in 1964 prior to California but nevertheless walked off with the nomination by dominating the caucus-conventions.[13] In the course of his run for the presidential nomination he voiced his opposition to federal civil rights legislation, a minimum wage, and a nuclear test ban treaty with the Soviet Union and came out in favor of voluntary social security, a military/economic blockade against Cuba, and allowing the commander of NATO to decide on the use nuclear weapons.[14]

It is also instructive that the Reverend Pat Robertson, representing the far right wing of the Republic party in his 1988 bid for the presidency, did not even come close to winning a single presidential primary. On the other hand, he won the first-round caucuses in Alaska, Hawaii, and Washington; came in second in two other caucuses, including the high-profile Iowa caucus; and, although not finishing first in the initial round of the Nevada caucus, ended up with the most delegates by the final round. The Reverend Jackson, who represented the far left wing of the Democratic party, managed to win seven state primaries, but the victories all came in places where blacks constituted no less than 19 percent of the population. In caucuses, meanwhile, Jackson managed to achieve victories in Alaska and Vermont, both states with few blacks, as well as in the state of Michigan, only 13 percent of whose population is black. Or consider the results in three states where Democrats had the opportunity to participate in both a primary and caucus. Michael Dukakis, the eventual Democratic nominee in 1988, won the nonbinding primary in Vermont with a turnout of 50,791, while Jackson won that state's caucus in which 6,000 participated. In Idaho's nonbinding primary, which brought out 51,242, Dukakis won with 73 percent of the vote, while managing no better than 38 percent of the caucus vote, in which only 4,633 participated. Finally, in the state of Texas, which uses both the primary and caucus to select delegates, Dukakis won the primary, in which a little over 1.7 million people voted, with 56% of the vote, but lost to Jackson in caucuses that brought out only 100,000 participants.[15]

MORE CANDIDATES

Prior to the reforms of the seventies and the concurrent proliferation of primaries, presidential aspirants who were not looked upon favorably by the party elites stood little chance of winning the nomination—a reality that no doubt discouraged many from even attempting to run. But changes in the nominating process, in conjunction with campaign finance reforms, have made it possible for candidates to take their cases directly to the American people via the primaries. It should not be surprising, then, that we find more candidates running for the presidency after 1968. In the three presidential elections prior to 1972, a total of twelve candidates ran for president in both parties, while in the three elections following 1968, a total of thirty-nine ran (see Table 3.2). Although the number of candidacies from 1972 to 2000 is understandably higher in the "out" party (i.e., the party not occupying the

Table 3.2.   Candidates for President in Both Parties, 1960–2000

Year	Democrats	Republicans
1960	4	2
1964	1	5
1968	5	4
1972	12	3
1976	12	2
1980	3	7
1984	8	1
1988	8	6
1992	6	3
1996	1	12
2000	2	11*

*This number includes the candidacy of Senator Robert Smith (N.H.) who initially announced as a Republican but subsequently changed his affiliation to independent.

presidency) and in years when an incumbent president is ineligible, even incumbent presidents have not always had a free ride. In 1976 President Ford had to fend off a serious challenge from Ronald Reagan; likewise, President Carter took seriously the challenges to his 1980 renomination by Senator Edward Kennedy and California governor Jerry Brown; and the rumblings about challenging Bill Clinton in 1996, following his party's loss of Congress in 1994, almost certainly would have become a reality had not the economy and his public approval ratings risen significantly as they did in 1996.

Of course, incumbents were not free of such challengers prior to the reforms. Henry Breckenridge decided to take on Franklin Roosevelt in 1936, and John Garner ran against him in 1940. Lyndon Johnson saw his presidency challenged in 1964 by George Wallace and four years later by Eugene McCarthy and Robert Kennedy. With the possible exception of 1968, however, none of these challenges was regarded as even remotely threatening to the incumbent.

The increase in the number of candidates running for the presidency is, on the whole, a healthy development in the nominating process. Within limits, more choice is better than less. Moreover, those who may not necessarily stand much chance of winning nevertheless have some opportunity to enter the national debate and, particularly in candidate forums, compel other contenders to address their concerns.

Some may argue that the proliferation of candidacies causes distracting background noise to the candidacies of major contenders. Perhaps, but those with virtually no national or regional following are typically eliminated even before the primaries start. Furthermore, notwithstanding the candidacy of Patrick Buchanan, the very permeability of the nominating process provides dissident groups with an incentive to compete *within* their parties, rather than against them as independent or third-party candidates.[16]

Some critics, however, have also pointed out that greater accessibility to the nominating process has left incumbent presidents more vulnerable to challenge from within their party, forcing them to divert their attention from more weighty matters of governing to the politics of their renomination.[17] While this argument has merit, it must be weighed against a competing consideration—namely, that the party leadership's firm control of the nominating process prior to 1972 virtually precluded any realistic challenge to an incumbent president. Harry Truman, for example, despite his low standing in the polls and even some disaffection in the Democratic party organization, faced no serious challenge to his renomination bid in 1948. (The same can be said of Herbert Hoover in 1932.) By 1952, disapproval of Truman's performance was even more widespread, and yet the evidence suggests that had he wanted it, the nomination would have been his once again. And even though the divisive effect of the Vietnam War rendered Johnson more vulnerable to challenge by McCarthy or Kennedy, his continued support among party leaders would probably have led to his renomination as well. Indeed, even after his disappointing performance in the New Hampshire primary, Democratic party leaders across the country were still convinced that Johnson would have carried 65 percent of the delegate vote at the 1968 Democratic convention.[18] The point here is not to argue that these presidents should or should not have been nominated for another term. Rather, it is to suggest that the process should not have foreclosed the opportunity to unseat them. Prior to the reforms, such challenges were all but impossible. Now they are not.

THE ORDEAL OF RUNNING

In 1960 John Kennedy and Richard Nixon declared for the presidency some six months before their parties' national conventions. This time frame would not have struck anyone as late in the game, since most delegates were then chosen by caucus or appointment, both of which were controlled by party leaders. While primaries were not usually ignored, they were entered selectively and viewed principally as a means of demonstrating voter appeal to party leaders. Kennedy, for example, entered only four contested primaries. In the 1952 Democratic race, Adlai Stevenson entered none.

With the party reforms and advent of the president-by-primary process, candidates must now take their case to a nationwide audience. This task, combined with the organizing that must be done to qualify for matching public funds, makes it virtually impossible to announce for the presidency six months before the conventions. On the contrary, candidates have been

declaring anywhere from twelve to eighteen months prior to their convention.[19] In the 2000 race for the presidency, the first Republican declaration
of candidacy came on February 19, 1999, and all but one of the remaining
candidates had done so by April 22, 1999. Nor do the formal declarations
tell the whole story, for many candidates have already been campaigning in-
formally months prior to throwing their hats into the ring. In the race of
1988, for example, candidates had been visiting Iowa for more than two years
prior to the year of its caucus, with Democratic candidates having logged
508 days there by January 1, 1988, and Republicans 296 days.[20]

As the contests begin, the pace quickens and the pressures grow. There
are interviews with the media, debates with opponents, countless speeches
before supporters, meetings with contributors, inevitable disputes within the
campaign staff, and a very great deal of travelling. Listen to Senator Edmund
Muskie (D-Me.) describe just one week in his 1972 bid for the presidential
nomination: "The previous week I'd been down to Florida, then I flew to
Idaho, then I flew to California, then I flew back to Washington to vote in
the Senate, and I flew back to California, and then I flew into Manchester
(New Hampshire)."[21] To all this must, of course, be added intense media
scrutiny, focusing not only on what candidates are saying and doing on the
campaign trail but also on what they may have done in the past, be it in their
public or private lives.

For the critics, what has just been described above is precisely the problem. They assert that the president-by-primary process, though long and
tortuous, does little to test candidates on the skills and qualities required in
the presidency. Furthermore, the campaign itself has become such an ordeal
that otherwise capable individuals are declining to run, thereby leaving the
field to those less accomplished:

> Participation in the embarrassing pageants we are now observing can be stom-
> ached only by second-raters. . . .
> Because the primaries have metastasized to the discredit of participatory de-
> mocracy, the time span of our quadrennial election orgy has been progressively
> extended to a point where the ordeal morally and physically demeans and de-
> pletes the candidates.[22]

> The primary system has made it so that nice guys, including the competent
> ones, stay out of the whole ordeal. Right from the start, the primary system
> means that only those who possess near psychopathic ambition and tempera-
> ment will get involved and stay involved.[23]

Several points should be noted in response to these indictments. First, the
presidency is the most demanding and consequential public office in the
world. Accordingly, a nominating process with formal and informal stages
that together consume the better part of two years does not seem inappropri-

ate to determine who shall be the nominees for that office. Furthermore, it is not unreasonable to assume that the longer we have to observe presidential candidates, the more of themselves they will reveal and the greater the likelihood that that they will be required to address not only what they have prepared for but also what they could not anticipate, be that the Soviet invasion of Afghanistan (1980), the death of a Soviet leader (1984), the stock market crash (1987), the Los Angeles riots following the Rodney King verdict (1992), or the commitment of U.S. troops into East Timor (1999).

Second, Bill Bradley aptly observed that "When you run for President, you've got to get your arms around the country in a very fundmental way."[24] Gruelling though it may be, the president-by-primary process is surely more successful than the old system in achieving that embrace, for it compels candidates to travel the length and breadth of the country, sensitizing them to its rich diversity as well as to issues on the minds of citizens in particular states and/or regions. Even Walter Mondale, two-time presidential candidate (1976, 1984), and scarcely a wholehearted enthusiast of the president-by-primary process, gives the current system its due on this point:

> The tremendous pressure and incredible schedules and fatigue and everything else that goes into a national campaign must be experienced to be believed. It takes an extraordinary or remarkable person to go through all that is necessary. And yet that very pressure and demanding schedule may be the most crucial test of one's ability to be a good President.
>
> A Presidential campaign requires a candidate to speak throughout the nation, to listen carefully, and to learn about the problems of regions and communities. All of this is an essential part of the education of potential Presidents about this country. I think only candidates can realize how incredibly vast and varied America is. It is only this way that candidates can become familiar with this country, with its people and their leaders, with its problems. In this way, they can come to respect the differences that exist in our country. And through this educational process a truly national leader, capable of dealing intelligently, responsibly and respectfully with our nation's problems, can be developed.[25]

Third, to suggest that the skills required to compete and win have little to do with those necessary to govern is not wholly accurate.[26] To be sure, some qualities many would value in a president, such as courage, decisiveness, or a sense of history, may not necessarily be tested; but then again, it is not altogether clear that they were under the old system either. Other qualities, however, get tested rather well—none more so than physical stamina and mental toughness (about which more shortly). There are others too, including a candidate's ability to identify, organize, motivate, and manage talent as he or she goes about the task of assembling an elaborate organization charged with waging a nationwide campaign. Also tested will be a candidate's mental dexterity and grasp of the major issues confronting the nation, for to a far greater extent than was true under the old system presidential candidates are subject to having their views probed and questioned by those best positioned to do so—their opponents. Between September 1987 and March 1988, for example, there were seventeen debates scheduled among Democratic candidates, ten among Republicans, and an additional two featuring candidates of both parties.[27] Approximately one-third were televised nationally and the remainder statewide. In the 1992 nomination race, there were five nationally televised debates among Democratic candidates from December 1991 through March 1992;[28] and in 1996, there were seven nationally televised debates among Republican presidential candidates between October 1995 and March 1996.[29] At this writing, Democratic presidential candidates Al Gore and Bill Bradley have already agreed to at least seven debates prior to the New Hampshire primary.

The current nominating process is also better suited than the old to preparing candidates for what has become an increasingly "public presidency."[30] It is more public in two respects, the first of which relates to exposure and the second to support.

Regarding the first, television has greatly expanded its commitment to news programming since 1963; the presidency is not only eminently newsworthy but also the easiest of the three national institutions to cover. Accordingly, presidents are covered more closely than ever before, and far outdistance Congress as the lead story on the evening news programs.[31] Moreover, in the aftermath of Vietnam and Watergate that coverage has become more intensely probing and critical, requiring of those who hold the office a toughness, temperament, and resilience of a very high order. The scrutiny to which candidates are exposed in the presidential selection process comes closest to replicating that experience. The president has also become increasingly dependant upon *public* support as a means of exerting leverage over those he seeks to persuade—a development made necessary by the declining importance of parties within Congress and the electorate.[32] Presidents who are particularly adept at projecting themselves on television (e.g. Reagan, Clinton) are also advantaged in their ability to generate that support. A television presence and skillful handling of the media is likewise of considerable importance to presidential candidates who, in the course of communicating with a host of primary electorates, must do so principally through the medium of television.

What of the claim that the president-by-primary process has become such a torture trail that it scares off many capable individuals, leaving the field to super-ambitious lesser lights? Some prominent Republicans mentioned as presidential timber do claim to have been put off by the process. Said William Bennett, member of both the Reagan and Bush administrations, "If you want everything you believe in to be caricatured, made fun of and belittled, then run for President."[33] (It is difficult, quite frankly, to imagine how the presidential office would afford him any respite from this sort of thing.) Richard Cheney, a former congressman and secretary of defense in the Bush administration, observed: "The more I thought about it, the more the process you have to subject yourself to weighed heavily on my mind. I concluded I was not prepared to pay the price."[34] And Jack Kemp, a former congressman and member of the Bush cabinet, volunteered that "my passion for ideas is not matched with a passion for partisan or electoral politics."[35] This aversion proved to be short-lived, however, as he accepted the offer to be Robert Dole's vice presidential running mate eighteen months later and in 1997 decided to create a candidate PAC for the 2000 race, noting that "My appetite is whetted."[36] Perhaps the most famous instance of a candidate being put off by the process was that of Walter Mondale. He actually entered the presidential race in 1976 and then withdrew, explaining, "I don't think anyone should be President who is not willing to go through the fire . . . I admire those with the determination to do what is required to seek the presidency, but I found I am not among them."[37] As with Kemp, however, he apparently overcame his misgivings about the process, and eight years later (1984) ran for and won the Democratic presidential nomination. Although the likelihood of winning the presidential nomination was not mentioned by any of these individuals as a factor in their decision to not run, or to withdraw, the skeptic can be forgiven for doubting that this consideration was very far from their minds.

Even if some presumably able individuals are discouraged from running *solely* because they find the process unattractive, it would be difficult to sustain the charge that it has failed to attract individuals of experience and accomplishment. On this point, the 1988 race deserves particular attention, for more so than in 1992 and 1996 the field was judged especially harshly when viewed against the "noncandidates" mentioned by the media and others. Among Republicans, those not running included former senators Howard Baker and Paul Laxalt, governors James Thompson and Thomas Kean, and former governor Lamar Alexander. On the Democratic side, those deciding not to run included senators Sam Nunn, Edward Kennedy, Dale Bumpers, and Bill Bradley, governors Mario Cuomo and Bill Clinton, and former governor Charles Robb.

Although the Democratic candidates were disparagingly characterized as the "seven dwarfs" in various media circles,[38] in terms of experience in public office, they compare favorably with the noncandidates in their party. Those announced candidates from the ranks of Congress (Gore, Simon, Gephardt, Biden, and Hart) had served between twelve and sixteen years in that body. Only noncandidate Senator Edward Kennedy served a substantially greater period of time. Meanwhile, the current or former Democratic governors running for president (Dukakis and Babbitt) served longer in that position than any noncandidate governor (Cuomo and Clinton). Not only was the Democratic field experienced but, as political columnist David Broder pointed out, they were also "serious government professionals, esteemed by their colleagues as unusually hard-working and engaged leaders."[39]

Except for evangelist Pat Robertson, experience in the Republican field was even more apparent. Jack Kemp had served in Congress for eighteen years. Robert Dole had twenty-seven years of congressional experience (six as Senate minority leader); he was also former chairman of the Republican National Committee and a former vice presidential nominee. George Bush held six different positions in government—congressman, chairman of the Republican National Committee, U. S. ambassador to the United Nations, director of the Central Intelligence Agency, chief of the U. S. Liaison office in China, and vice president. Pierre Dupont had been an eight-year governor, and Alexander Haig had served in the executive branch for some ten years, mostly in the White House, followed by a brief tenure as secretary of state. Although three of the Republican noncandidates (Baker, Laxalt, and Thompson) had served in government longer than Dupont and Haig, none had logged as much time as Bush, Dole, and Kemp.

To be sure, none of the announced candidates in either party was wholly lacking in liabilities, as their opponents and a watchful media were only too willing to point out. On the other hand, we should also bear in mind that the major reason "noncandidates" so often come off more favorably when contrasted with those running is precisely because their past records have not yet been subject to the scrutiny of national media and declared candidates.

If the reformed nominating process attracts capable individuals running for president, it must also be acknowledged that those ranks have included individuals with little or no experience in public office who never would have made it into the race under the old system—Jesse Jackson (1988), Pat Robertson (1988), Patrick Buchanan (1992, 1996, 2000), Alan Keyes (1996, 2000), and Maurice Taylor (1996). But we should expect such candidacies in a nominating process that is far more open than it used to be. The more important question is: how far did they get? Not a single one has even come close to winning the presidential nomination. Taylor and Keyes did not even register in the national poll ratings and won no contests. Robertson managed to win three caucuses but not a single primary. Jackson's hard-core support in the black community enabled him to win seven primaries and seven caucuses, but his inability to significantly expand that base into the white community left him with little chance of winning. Buchanan's populist message struck a nerve with a certain portion of the electorate in 1996, giving him a win in the important New Hampshire primary, albeit with a plurality of only 27 percent. But nearly half of his own party saw him as an "extremist," and once the field was narrowed following the New Hampshire primary, those who had supported other candidates did not turn to Buchanan.[40] He won no more primaries thereafter and a total of only three caucuses. He has thrown his hat into the ring yet again for the 2000 race, but his inability to attract much support, financial or otherwise, in the Republican party sent him searching for greener pastures in Ross Perot's Reform Party.

THE RUBBER STAMP CONVENTION

When delegates convened at the 1960 Democratic National Convention, most were not legally bound to vote for a given candidate, and many were not even required to express a presidential preference when their names were listed on the ballot in their state's presidential primary. As noted in the first chapter, however, the independence enjoyed by these delegates was gradually eroded by reforms implemented between 1971 and 1978. The first move in this direction came in 1971, when the McGovern–Fraser Commission required that delegates selected by the primary method be given the opportunity to express a presidential preference (including "uncommitted"), unless state law prohibited them from doing so. The Mikulski Commission went even further in 1974 by requiring that all delegates chosen in caucuses and primaries state their presidential preference. Where state law prohibited such declarations parties were required to publicize in the newspapers names of delegates, along with their presidential preference. Furthermore, presidential candidates were allowed to approve all delegates intending to support them. In 1978, the Winograd Commission required that delegates vote for their stated presidential preference on the first ballot and authorized presidential candidates to replace any delegate who was disloyal. Known as the "yank rule," it generated considerable debate at the 1980 Democratic convention, leading the Hunt Commission to recommend its repeal.

The critics charge that the president-by-primary process has fundamentally transformed the convention from a deliberative body to merely a rubber stamp for decisions already made in the caucuses and the primaries.[41]

Whether the conventions were ever as deliberative as the critics would have us believe is open to question. Writing as far back as 1940, one of the most astute observers of American politics observed that "To expect bands of local chieftains and their henchmen to come together and act as a deliberative national unit every four years is to expect the impossible."[42] Moreover, as Warren Carlton notes in a classic piece on presidential nominating conventions, "after 1924 the convention of each party has picked a national favorite—usually *the* national favorite—as the presidential nominee."[43] There would not appear to be much deliberation there.

Bound or unbound, it is even more improbable that delegates to the 2000 Democratic National Convention, for example, could deliberate in any *collective* sense if only because their numbers are so great—4,976 as compared to 1,521 in 1960 and 1,154 in 1940. On the other hand, the critics did have a point in noting that the binding rule impedes *individual* deliberation. In a nominating process that runs over several months, it is possible that a presidential candidate who appeared strong at the start of the process might look very weak at the end. Delegates should be able to factor this abrupt change of circumstances into their voting decision; they have in fact had the ability to do so since the adoption of the Hunt Commission reforms in 1982. Dispensing with the previous language *requiring* delegates to vote for their stated preference on the first ballot, the Democratic Party replaced it with far more ambiguous wording that states that "delegates elected to the national convention pledged to a presidential candidate shall in all good conscience reflect the sentiments of those who elected them."[44] It is true, of course, that candidates continue to have the authority to approve delegates who intend to support them, and thus it is not likely that delegates could be easily divorced from that commitment. On the other hand, if by virtue of behavior or revelation, a presidential candidacy were dealt a severe blow, causing a significant national decline in public support, convention delegates would certainly be free "in all good conscience" to reflect that change in sentiment when voting on the convention floor.

DIMINISHED PARTY ELITES

Of all the deficiencies ascribed to the president-by-primary process, none perhaps resonates more strongly with its critics than the diminished role of the party elites in the choosing of presidential nominees. Political scientist James Sundquist exemplifies this concern:

> When the state primaries became the mode rather than the exception after 1968, a basic safeguard in the presidential election process was lost. Previously an elite of party leaders performed a screening function. They administered a kind of competence test; they did not always exercise the duty creditably, but they could—and did—ensure that no one was nominated who was not acceptable to the preponderance of the party elite as its leader. Even if the candidate swept the limited number of primaries, he could still be rejected, as Senator Estes Kefauver was in 1952. Usually, then, the nominee was a politician or an administrator, or both, of national stature and of demonstrated competence. The party leaders who approved the nomination were prepared to follow the nominee, and to mobilize the party on his behalf.

Once again, the critics have overstated their case, for the influence of the party elites, although undeniably reduced, can still make itself felt in the current nominating process. Furthermore, the important quality-control function they are presumed to have performed under the old system was actually less impressive than some would have us believe. We shall now address each of these points in turn.

As noted in the first chapter, a certain number of convention slots have been reserved for superdelegates—party officials and public office holders who, if they choose, may go to the Democratic National Convention uncommitted to any candidate. While their initial number was set at 14 percent of the delegates to the 1984 convention, the percentage was raised to 15.5 percent for 1988, 18 percent for 1992, and 20 percent for 1996. It should be noted, however, that while superdelegates constituted 20 percent of all delegates to the 1996 national convention, they represented fully 36 percent of the number needed for nomination. Thus, if united, superdelegates could make the difference in a relatively close contest, as indeed they did in the 1984 nomination race. Still shy of the needed majority following the final round of primaries on June 5, Mondale appealed to fellow members of Congress, many of whom were superdelegates, and they provided the margin of votes needed to put him over the top.[46]

Although the Republican party has no superdelegates, elements of the party elite nevertheless provided valuable support to Robert Dole in his 1996 bid for the presidency. Ironically, that support proved most beneficial precisely because of the "front-loading" of primaries. Coming out of the New Hampshire primary having lost to Patrick Buchanan, it was crucial that Dole re-establish momentum with a win. Following New Hampshire, the primaries came in rapid succession, making it difficult for Buchanan, who lacked the resources, to field an organization in most of these primary states. Dole, however, was able to do so because he received the endorsement of twenty-seven Republican governors, all of whom placed their state party organizations at his disposal in the primaries.[47] Nowhere was that advantage more apparent than in the states of South Carolina and New York; nowhere was it more crucial than in South Carolina.

Frustrated by having been shut out of the White House for eight years, the Republican elites have weighed in early and heavily for someone they think can win, notably, George W. Bush. As of this writing, and with nearly a year to go before the first primary, over half the Republican governors have endorsed him, along with 117 members of the U.S. House of Representatives, 5 members of the U.S. Senate, and a majority of state legislators in California, North Carolina, and South Carolina.[48] How this support helps Bush down the road remains to be seen, but at this early stage it cannot help but enhance his credibility, and therefore his ability to raise unprecedented sums of money as well.

What of the quality-control function that has been attributed to the party elites? Here, the promise has outpaced the reality. Writing about the American political system in the late 1800s, Alfred Bryce noted that "what a party wants is not a good president but a good candidate. . . . The Party managers have therefore to look out for the person likely to gain most support and at the same time excite the least opposition."[49] While he may have overstated the case, the fact remains that political parties unable to win elections are failing in their primary reason for being. Accordingly, it should not be altogether surprising that from 1936 through 1968, during which time the party elites controlled the nominating process, the national conventions on all but one occasion nominated the *candidate most preferred by the rank and file of their party.*[50] This datum would seem to suggest either that the rank and file were fully as discerning as the party elites or the party elites were fully as unenlightened as the rank and file. In either case, the screening function of the party elites would appear to be problematic. Let us also consider the one instance where the choice of the party elites did in fact diverge from that of their party rank and file. Senator Estes Kefauver (D-Ark.) came into the 1952 Democratic convention having entered thirteen of seventeen primaries and having won twelve. He also enjoyed a decisive lead in the polls (Kefauver, 45 percent; Stevenson, 12 percent; Russell, 10 percent; Harriman, 5 percent).[51] Stevenson, however, was the clear preference of the party elites, and consequently Kefauver was passed over for the nomination. Not surprisingly, Stevenson went on to lose in the general election against Eisenhower. The decision to reject Kefauver, however, was not rooted in the belief that he was not presidential timber. Indeed, one longtime chronicler of presidential elections opined that "he seemed most qualified for the leadership denied him."[52] Rather, the party leadership's rejection of Kefauver appears to have been motivated primarily by the fact that his Senate crime committee hearings had unearthed connections between some big-city Democratic party machines and organized crime. To make matters worse, he also lost favor with Truman for declaring his candidacy before the president had made clear his own intentions regarding another term.[53]

If party elites seemed heavily inclined to follow the polls under the old system, it cannot be said that superdelegates have behaved much differently under the new. In circumstances when poll and/or primary results have been ambiguous, most superdelegates have held back committing themselves to a candidate. By the same token, when the front-runner appeared to be the likely nominee, the superdelegates have jumped on board in advance of the convention.[54] As of this writing Vice President Al Gore has experienced some difficulty rounding up commitments from congressional superdelegates—not surprising, given the stronger-than-anticipated showing by presidential hopeful Bill Bradley in both polls and fund-raising and Gore's poor showing in trial heats against George W. Bush. In the words of Senator Joseph Biden (D-Del.) "Even if he (Gore) gets them to commit, these guys will stampede in a second if Bill Bradley wins New Hampshire."[55] George W. Bush, on the other hand, has been way ahead of other Republican candidates in both the polls and raising money. Accordingly, roughly two out of three

Republican governors and members of Congress have leapt onto the Bush bandwagon, and according to representative Roy Blunt (R-Mo.), House Republican chief deputy whip, "Frankly, a lot of our members endorsed him before they met him. . . ."[56] All this eight months or more before a single primary, caucus, or debate has been held.[57] For those who entertain some skepticism regarding the discernment ascribed to party elites, this rush to judgment is not altogether reassuring.

The critics, of course, argue that the proof of the pudding is in the eating, pointing out as one did that "The old rules—the old bosses—gave us Franklin Delano Roosevelt. The new rules gave us McGovern, Carter, and Reagan."[58] Accordingly, it is worth considering at some length the individuals who have been nominated under the president-by-primary process.

Although McGovern, Carter, and Reagan have been mentioned as examples of misfirings in the president-by-primary process, it should first be noted that the latter two would in all likelihood have been nominated even under the old system. Carter did, after all, come into the convention with a hefty 53 percent of rank-and-file Democrats favoring his nomination. Reagan, meanwhile, had led in the polls since September of 1978 and arrived at the convention with 46 percent of Republican identifiers supporting his nomination; and, of course, he went on to win by a landslide in the general election. McGovern, on the other hand, almost certainly would not have been chosen. Coming into the convention, he led in the polls with a plurality of only 30 percent and espoused views that Democratic party elites found objectionable.[59]

Fear that the demise of the party elites would invite self-starting, insurgent candidates with little experience to ride the primary waves to nomination and the White House simply has not materialized. As Gerald Pomper observes, "Since 1980 . . . we have seen ten presidential nominations, all of them the choice of an established party leader, even in the face of significant insurgencies. These selections include four renominations of the sitting party leader, with only one facing a strong challenge (Carter, 1980); four selections of the leader of the established dominant faction of the party; and two selections of the leader of a major party faction."[60]

Furthermore, if we compare the government experience of those chosen by the president-by-primary process to those elevated to the nomination under the old system, the former compare favorably with the latter. Table 3.4 shows the nominees of both parties chosen in the seven elections since 1968 and also nominees selected in the seven elections prior to 1972.

Those chosen after 1968 had a total of 149 years of prior government experience at the national and state (i.e., governorship) level, with 16.5 years as the average number logged by these individuals. Those first-time nominees in the seven elections prior to 1972 served a total of 137 years, with the average number of years in service coming to 13.7. Even if we include in this

Table 3.3.   Recent Presidential Nominations

Year	Party	Candidate	Type
1980	Dem.	Carter	Renomination of incumbent
1980	Rep.	Reagan	Dominant factional victory
1984	Dem.	Mondale	Dominant factional victory
1984	Rep.	Reagan	Renomination of incumbent
1988	Dem.	Dukakis	Factional victory
1992	Dem.	Clinton	Factional victory
1992	Rep.	Bush	Renomination of incumbent
1996	Dem.	Clinton	Renomination of incumbent
1996	Rep.	Dole	Dominant factional victory

Source: Gerald M. Pomper, "Parliamentary Government in the U.S.?" in *The State of the Parties,* 3rd edition, eds. John C. Green and Daniel M. Shea (Lanham, Md.: Rowman & Littlefield, 1999), p. 266.

group Eisenhower's approximately six years of service as allied commander, supreme allied commander, and army chief of staff, then the total number of years comes out to 143, with an average of 14.3 years of government service prior to receiving the presidential nomination. Were we to look further back than 1944, the prior government experience of post-1968 nominees would very likely look even better. As two of our most eminent historians (Samuel Elliot Morrison and Henry Steele Commager) noted, writing back in 1930: "Since 1840 successful presidential candidates have not been prominent and experienced statesmen, but military heroes or relatively obscure men who have not had time to make enemies. Only by inadvertence, as in the case of Lincoln or the Roosevelts, did the president prove to be a man of outstanding ability."[61]

While it is certainly true that none of the individuals nominated from 1944 through 1968 had as few years in the harness as Jimmy Carter prior to receiving the nomination, we should not overlook the context in which he ran. Having recently weathered the greatest political scandal surrounding the presidency and a pardon of the man responsible for it, the nation's receptivity to a candidacy from *outside* of Washington was particularly strong in 1976. Furthermore, the old system gave us nominees whose prior experience in government was not especially noteworthy either. Woodrow Wilson had only served three years as governor of New Jersey. Franklin Roosevelt was governor of New York for one term and prior to that served eight years as assistant secretary of the navy. In assessing the Roosevelt candidacy, the leading scholar/journalist of the time (Walter Lippman) characterized him as "a pleasant man who, without any important qualifications for the office, would very much like to be president."[62] Adlai Stevenson also served just one term as Illinois governor, following brief stints in the departments of

Table 3.4. Presidential Nominees: Government Experience (in years) Prior to
First Presidential Nomination, 1944–1996

Election	Nominee	Prior Government Experience			Total Yrs.
		Exec.	Cong.	Govn'r	
1996	Dole		34		34
1992	Clinton			13	13
1988	Bush	15	5		20
1988	Dukakis			10	10
1984	Mondale	4	13		17
1980	Reagan			8	8
1976	Carter			4	4
1976	Ford	2	25		27
1972	McGovern		16		16
					149
1968	Humphrey	4	16		20
1964	Johnson	3	24		27
1964	Goldwater		12		12
1960	Kennedy		14		14
1960	Nixon	8	6		14
1952	Eisenhower	0	0	0	0
1952	Stevenson	7		4	11
1948	Truman	4	10		14
1944	F. Roosevelt	8	4		12
1944	Dewey			13	13
					137

Agriculture and State, where he occupied several junior positions. Scarcely a national political figure, he was described by one close student of American politics as emerging "from truly outer darkness as the Democratic candidate."[63] And in the same year Stevenson was nominated by the Democrats, Dwight Eisenhower, with no prior political experience in civilian life, was nominated by the Republicans.

Of the individuals whose *first* nomination to the presidency came under the president-by-primary process, five (Ford, Carter, Reagan, Bush, and Clinton) went on to win the presidency. Although more tempered judgments of their tenure in office must await the passage of time, initial assessments suggest that as a group they acquitted themselves reasonably well.

Gerald Ford assumed the reins of power at a particularly traumatic moment, and the essential decency he brought to that challenge provided a welcome change from his predecessor. In the face of a more assertive Congress populated by huge Democratic majorities—both results of the Watergate scandals—Ford's room to maneuver was severely constrained. Yet there were some achievements and no grave missteps. Two festering wounds, Watergate and Vietnam, he sought to put behind us by granting a pardon to Richard Nixon and clemency to draft evaders and deserters. He also threw his support behind legislation calling for campaign finance reform, extension of the Voting Rights Act, and consumer protection. In foreign policy, his administration achieved the Helsinki Agreement (1975), which constructed an architecture for subsequent relations between the United States and the Soviet Union.

Leaving Carter aside for the moment, Ronald Reagan won two terms as president and, as even his critics acknowledge, left the office much stronger than he found it: "Whatever else may be said about Ronald Reagan, he quickly showed that reports of the death of the presidency were greatly exaggerated."[64] Although scholars vigorously debate the wisdom of some Reagan policies, his role in redefining the national agenda was profound. In his majesterial work on the presidency, Stephen Skowronek speaks to this point: "No president in recent times has so radically altered the terms in which prior governmental commitments are now dealt with or the conditions under which previously established interests are served."[65] Another eminent scholar of American politics is no less sweeping in his assessment: "The true extent and success of the 'Reagan revolution' will remain matters for debate for some time to come. But few would deny that he made more of a difference—not only in changing the playing field itself—than all but a few presidents in this century."[66]

Although George Bush's presidency would ultimately fall victim to a downturn in the business cycle, he skillfully managed the potentially explosive savings and loan crisis and concluded his presidency with inflation at 3 percent and interest rates the lowest in two decades. It was in the foreign policy area, however, that his leadership talents were most apparent. In a period of uncertainty following the end of the Cold War, he deftly forged and held together a coalition of diverse countries that, in the most extensive military undertaking since the Vietnam War, successfully drove Saddam Hussein's forces out of Kuwait; he convinced hesitant European nations to support the historic reunification of Germany; and he signed a treaty with the Soviet Union calling for unprecedented reductions in nuclear weaponry.

Bill Clinton not only managed to win two terms but was the first Democratic president to do so since Franklin Roosevelt, and he won at a time when the opposition party was dominant in presidential elections. During his stewardship, he has presided over the longest economic expansion in our nation's history,[67] secured passage of important legislation in the areas of trade (NAFTA, GATT), crime prevention, deficit reduction, and national service, and appointed more women and minorities to important government positions than any president in history. No recent president has displayed a greater mastery of the issues or explained them with such fluency. He was, of course, also impeached by a process that, though fatally undermined by bitter partisanship, was nevertheless brought on by the president's exceedingly poor judgment in matters related to his private life. His womanizing, however, was well known to voters and politicians before he was elected, *and* to superdelegates in the Democratic Party, who showed little inclination to weigh in against him on this count. Nor, incidentally, did his own self-indulgent behavior remotely approach the recklessness exhibited by John Kennedy's dalliances—not unknown to those in political circles—both before and during his presidency;[68] nor finally, and most importantly, was the incaution manifest in Clinton's private life anywhere apparent in his public role as president. On the contrary, his decision-making style was faulted not for precipitous action but rather for labored deliberation.[69]

Jimmy Carter's presidency is generally regarded as the least successful of those in the post-reform period and, in the view of the critics, illustrative of the kind of presidents who can emerge from the president-by-primary process. In the words of political columnist David Broder, "The point is as long as we have this kind of selection process, his is the kind of presidency we are going to get."[70] A Washington outsider of limited political experience, his presidency was said to evidence both of these limitations. He had few close ties to members of Congress, surrounded himself with White House aides lacking in Washington experience, did not pick his fights wisely, and failed to convey to other powerholders what really mattered to him. But even though these deficiencies made for a rocky presidency, particularly early on, his stewardship was not, as some would suggest, a failure.[71] A more sober assessment of his record is made by Stephen Skowronek:

> For all the attention that has been lavished on Carter's inexperience with the ways of Washington and his incompetence in making the government work, he still got a lot done. He was well within the ballpark of legislative performance for modern presidents, and like them, he had notable accomplishments to boast all along the way: the creation of the Department of Energy, government reorganization, the Panama Canal treaties, the normalization of relations with China, the creation of the Department of Education, the overhaul of the civil service system, two energy conservation packages, the negotiation of a strategic arms limitation treaty, the deregulation of transportation and banking, stiffer regulation of strip mining and off-shore drilling, the Egypt–Israel accord, a renewed commitment to national defense.[72]

Even if Carter, or any of the other post-reform presidents, had been an abject failure in office, this fact would not necessarily constitute compelling grounds for restoring the influence of the party elites. There were, after all, some notable misfirings under the old system. It was the party elites who gave us Warren Harding, arguably the worst president in our nation's history. They also rewarded Herbert Hoover, rated by many scholars as a "failure" in office,[73] with renomination, even though his first four years scarcely justified such confidence. More recently, we have the case of Richard Nixon who, along with Franklin Roosevelt, is the only individual in the history of this republic ever to be nominated for national office five times—twice for vice president and three times for president. In each of his three presidential bids, he commanded the support of the Republican party's rank and file *and its leadership.* Once again, we were not well served by the screening function of the party elites, despite the fact that his previous track record in politics ought to have invited considerable skepticism among those presumed to be most discerning in identifying presidential timber.[74] Almost a quarter century after his service in office, he is still regarded by many scholars as a failed president.[75]

NOMINATING AND GOVERNING

Those harboring serious doubts about the efficacy of the current nominating process also insist that it complicates a president's ability to govern.[76] Under the old system, it is argued, presidential candidates were required to forge alliances and reach accommodations with party elites—the very people they would have to share power with once they became president. The bonds forged in the crucible of nomination politics would carry over into the politics of governing, enhancing the president's ability to work his will. With the demise of the party elites in the nominating process, according to the critics, presidential candidates are no longer obliged to take their views into account, which presumably renders more difficult their ability to govern.

That segment of the party elite most crucial to a president's success in governing is members of Congress, since most of what he wants to do will require their support in one way or another. Yet the critics have not provided much in the way of specifics as to how these alliances with members of Congress were forged under the old system, what accomodations were reached, and the implications of both for the president's policy positions. More importantly, recent evidence suggests that the disconnect between presidential candidates and the congressional wing of their party, presumed to be a consequence of the president-by-primary process, is not quite as apparent as the critics seem to suggest. In a detailed study covering the period 1952–1992, Kelly Patterson compares the policy positions of congressional leaders of each party with their presidential nominees. Although the average rates of agreement for the entire period would appear to be relatively low—12 percent for Democrats and 9 percent for Republicans—he found that

the percentage of agreement between Democratic candidates and the Democratic congressional leaders actually is greater and more consistent from 1972 to

1992 than in the earlier era. The percentage of agreement in 1976 (19%), 1980 (14%), 1992 (19%) are three of the four largest rates of agreement documented and are comparable to the largest percentage from the pre-reform era, which was 18% in 1960 . . . If electoral and governing coalitions were actually splitting as a result of reforms in the party system since 1972, the results for 1976, 1980, and 1992 are counter to what we would expect.[77]

If, as the critics suggest, the old nominating process forged closer bonds between presidential candidates and the congressional wing of their party, then we should also expect those elected prior to 1972, as a group, to be more successful in uniting their party behind them than those elected after 1968. John Bond and Richard Fleisher have examined the legislative success of presidents from Dwight Eisenhower to Ronald Reagan (first term), and included in their analysis the percentage of time a president's party base was unifed (defined as at least 75 percent) in support of him on "important votes." Although the small number of post-reform presidents included here precludes us from confidently drawing conclusions one way or the other, the results are nevertheless suggestive. In examining the House first, Kennedy (95 percent) and Johnson (92 percent), both nominated under the old system, finish well ahead of the others. On the other hand, Reagan (68 percent), Ford (68 percent), and Carter (61 percent) finish comfortably ahead of Nixon (57 percent) and Eisenhower (53 percent), who were also chosen by the old system. In the Senate, Kennedy (85 percent) once again finishes first, followed by Ford (82 percent) and Nixon (78 percent). Reagan (72 percent) falls in the middle of the pack, just ahead of Johnson (71 percent) and comfortably in front of Eisenhower (64 percent). Carter (55 percent), meanwhile, finishes in last place.[78] In sum, the first four finishers in each group include two presidents chosen under the old system and two chosen under the new. To be sure, in regard to party support in the House, the top two finishers (Kennedy and Johnson) chosen under the old nominating process finished well ahead of Reagan, Ford, and Carter. In weighing these differences, however, several points must be kept in mind. Kennedy's percentage is inflated, for many of the most important votes on his legislation came after his death, with Johnson as president.[79] Add to this the fact that Kennedy's death itself provided a galvinizing force for uniting Democrats in Congress. Furthermore, Reagan had more than double the number of important votes (151) as Kennedy (65), and Carter nearly double (113). Finally, in contrast to their predecessors, Ford, Carter, and Reagan served during the time when, as a consequence of reforms and changes within Congress, the task of lining up support among party members posed a greater challenge than either Kennedy or Johnson confronted.[80]

CONCLUSION

At bottom, there are two characteristics of the president-by-primary process that distinguish it from its predecessor. First, the selection of presidential nominees is placed in the hands of primary electorates rather than party elites, although the latter still have an opportunity to have an impact on the process. Second, expensive and demanding though it may be, the president-by-primary process subjects candidates to more protracted and intense scrutiny by the public, media, and even the party elites, than ever occurred under the old system. To be sure, this scrutiny does not guarantee that the most qualified candidate will be chosen. No system can. Yet it probably does a better job than the old system of ensuring that we do not select a very bad candidate. Certainly the president-by-primary process has not yet nominated a candidate whose views were as decidedly at variance with a majority of Americans as were those of Barry Goldwater (1964). Nor has it produced a nominee whose overall level of competence was as lacking as Warren Harding's (1920). Nor finally, has it given us a president whose insensitivity to constitutional requirements approached that of Richard Nixon (1960, 1968, 1972).

NOTES

1. Robert A. Dahl, "Myth of a Presidential Mandate," *Political Science Quarterly* 105 (Fall 1990), p. 368.

2. *Washington Post,* June 8, 1980, B7.

3. Terry Sanford, *A Danger of Democracy: The Presidential Nominating Process* (Boulder, Colo.: Westview, 1981), p. 101.

4. For a discussion of the unsuccessful attempts by the chairman of the Democratic National Committee to keep the New Hampshire primary within the window in the 1984 nomination race see Charles Brereton, *First in the Nation: New Hampshire and the Premier Presidential Primary* (Portsmouth, N.H.: Peter E. Randall, 1987), pp. 221–223.

5. Tami Buhr, "What Voters Know about the Candidates and How They Learn It: The 1996 New Hampshire Republican Primary as a Case Study," in *In Pursuit of the White House 2000: How We Choose Our Presidential Nominees,* ed., William G. Mayer, (New York: Chatham House, Publishers, 2000), pp. 224, 228, 229, 232, 233.

6. *Congressional Quarterly Weekly Report,* June 15, 1996, p. 1704; *Congressional Quarterly Weekly Report,* August 3, 1996, p. 62.

7. Austin Ranney, *Participation in American Presidential Nominations, 1976* (Washington, D.C.: American Enterprise Institute, 1977), p. 15.

8. *Wall Street Journal,* August 13, 1979, p. 14. See also Edward Banfield, "Party Reform in Retrospect," in *Political Parties in the Eighties,* ed. Robert A. Goldwin, (Washington, D.C.: American Enterprise Institute, 1980), p. 27; Byron Shafer, "Anti-Party Politics," *The Public Interest* 63 (Spring, 1981), p. 101.

9. James I. Lengle. *Representation and Presidential Primaries: The Democratic Party in the Post-Reform Era* (Westport, Conn.: Greenwood Press, 1981). Even this study must be viewed with some caution as it was confined only to the California primary.

10. Barbara G. Farah, "Convention Delegates: Party Reform and the Representativeness of Party Elites, 1972–1980." (Prepared for delivery at the Annual Meeting of the American Political Science Association, New York, September 3–6, 1981), pp. 3, 7, 9, 11. See also results of a *New York Times*/CBS News poll in *New York Times,* October 30, 1995, A10; John G. Geer, "The Represensentativeness of Presidential Primary Electorates." (Prepared for delivery at Annual Meeting of the American Political Science Association, New Orleans, August 29–September 1, 1985), p. 28; Herbert M. Kritzer, "The Representativeness of the 1972 Presidential Primaries," in *The Party Symbol,* ed., William Crotty (San Francisco, W. H. Freeman, 1980), pp. 148–152.

11. Barbara Norrander, "Ideological Represensentativeness of Presidential Primary Voters," *American Journal of Political Science* 33 (August 1989), pp. 570–587.

12. See, for example, *Washington Post,* October 2, 1981, A6; *Washington Post,* January 18, 1981, A14; *Dominion Post,* November 8, 1992, 5a;

13. Sanford, *A Danger of Democracy,* p. 25.

14. Benjamin I. Page, *Choices and Echoes in Presidential Elections: Rational Man and Electoral Democracy* (Chicago: University of Chicago Press, 1978), pp. 122–124.

15. *Congressional Quarterly Weekly Report,* June 4, 1988, pp. 1523–1527.

16. On this point see Benjamin Ginsberg, *The Consequences of Consent: Elections, Citizen Control, and Popular Acquiescence* (Reading, Mass.: Addison-Wesley, 1982), pp. 148–150.

17. See, for example, Robert S. Hirschfield, ed., *Selection/Election: A Forum on the American Presidency* (New York: Aldine Publishing Co., 1982), p. 168; Richard E. Neustadt, *Presidential Power: The Politics of Leadership from FDR to Carter* (New York: Wiley, 1980), pp. 175, 176.

18. William Keech and Donald Matthews, *The Party's Choice* (Washington, D.C.: Brookings Institution, 1976), pp. 40–42, 106.

19. Harold W. Stanley and Richard G. Niemi, *Vital Statistics on American Politics* (Washington D.C.: Congressional Quarterly Press, 1988), p. 73.

20. *Washington Post,* January 8, 1988, A4.

21. Cited in Theodore White, *The Making of the President 1972* (New York: Atheneum, 1973), p. 81.

22. George Ball, "Unnatural Selection," *Washington Post,* February 29, 1980, A13.

23. Cited in Anthony King, "How Not to Select Presidents: A View from Europe," in *The American Elections of 1980,* ed. Austin Ranney, (Washington, D.C.: American Enterprise Institute, 1981), pp. 321, 322.

24. Cited in Melinda Henneberger, "The Aura of the Aura," *New York Times Magazine,* June 27, 1999, p. 29.

25. Walter F. Mondale, *The Accountability of Power: Toward a Responsible Presidency* (New York: David McKay, 1975), pp. 259, 260.

26. See, for example, *Washington Post,* March 29, 1987, C2.

27. *Washington Post,* September 8, 1987, A10.

28. Television News Archive, "Search Special Reports & Periodic Broadcasts 1991, 1992" Vanderbilt University, <http://tvnews.vanderbilt.edu> 1/6/99, 11:47 AM.

29. Television News Archive, "Search Special Reports & Periodic Broadcasts 1996," Vanderbilt University, <http://tvnews.vanderbilt.edu> 1/6/99, 11:45 AM; Television News Archive, "Special Reports & Periodic Broadcasts 1995," Vanderbilt University, <http://tvnews.vanderbilt.edu> 8/6/99, 9:01 AM.

30. See, for example, Samuel Kernell, *Going Public: New Strategies of Presidential Leadership,* 3rd Edition (Washington, D.C.: Congressional Quarterly Press, 1997).

31. Robert E. Gilbert, "President versus Congress: The Struggle for Public Attention," *Congress and the Presidency* 16 (1989), pp. 86, 87.

32. Kernell, *Going Public,* pp. 1–64.

33. Cited in *New York Times,* February 5, 1995, E1.

34. Cited in *Congressional Quarterly Weekly Report,* January 4, 1996, p. 175.

35. Cited in *Washington Post,* January 31, 1995, A5.

36. Cited in *Washington Post,* February 10, 1997, A7.

37. Cited in Arthur Hadley, *The Invisible Primary* (Englewood Cliffs, N.J.: Prentice-Hall, 1976), p. 38.

38. *Washington Post,* September 9, 1987, A21.

39. *Washington Post,* March 25, 1987, A23.

40. William G. Mayer, "The Presidential Nominations," in *The Election of 1996: Reports and Interpretations,* ed. Gerald M. Pomper, et al., (Chatham, N.J.: Chatham House, 1996), pp. 53, 54.

41. Jeane Kirkpatrick, et al., The Presidential Nominating Process: Can It Be Improved? (Washington, D.C.: American Enterprise Institute, 1980), p. 14.

42. Pendleton Herring, *The Politics of Democracy: American Parties in Action* (New York: W. W. Norton, 1940), p. 225.

43. Warren G. Carlton, "The Revolution in the Presidential Nominating Convention," *Political Science Quarterly* 71 (June, 1957), pp. 224–240; quoted in Roger Davidson, "Brokered Conventions Are Not Desirable," in *Controversial Issues in Presidential Selection,* ed. Gary L. Rose (Albany: SUNY Press, 1994), p. 69.

44. *Report of the Commission on Presidential Nomination* (Washington, D.C.: Democratic National Committee, 1982), p. 46.

45. James Sundquist, "The Crisis of Competence in Government," in *Setting National Priorities: Agenda for the 1980s,* ed. Joseph Pechman (Washington, D.C.: Brookings Institution, 1980), p. 543.

46. *Congressional Quarterly Weekly Report,* April 25, 1992, p. 1083; Priscilla Southwell. "The 1984 Democratic Nominating Process: The Significance of Unpledged Superdelegates," *American Politics Quarterly* 14 (January/April, 1986), pp. 75–88.

47. *Washington Post,* March 15, 1996, A14.

48. *Washington Post,* March 7, 1999, A6; *Washington Post,* June 9, 1999, A6.

49. James Bryce, *The American Commonwealth,* vol. 1 (London: Macmillan, 1889), p. 187.

50. William H. Lucy, "Polls, Primaries, and Presidential Nominations," *Journal of Politics* 35 (November 1973), p. 837.

51. Keech and Matthews, *The Party's Choice,* p. 185; George Gallup, *The Gallup*

Opinion Poll: Public Opinion, 1935–1971, vol. 2 (New York: Random House, 1972), p. 1075.

52. Theodore White, *America in Search of Itself, 1956–1980* (New York: Harper and Row, 1982), p. 75.

53. James W. Davis, *Presidential Primaries: Road to the White House* (New York: Thomas Y. Crowell, 1967), p. 176.

54. *New York Times,* April 10, 1992, A16; *National Journal,* July 9, 1988, p. 1838; *Congressional Quarterly Weekly Report,* July 4, 1992, p. 18.

55. Quoted in *Washington Post,* September 10, 1999, A5. See also *New York Times,* September 15, 1999, p. 18.

56. Cited in *New York Times,* October 10, 1999, p. 20.

57. *New York Times,* September 15, 1999, p. 18.

58. Hirschfield, *Selection/Election,* p. 107.

59. *The Gallup Opinion Index,* December 1980, report no. 183, pp. 13, 16; Gerald M. Pomper, et al., The Election of 1980: Reports and Interpretations (Chatham, N.J.: Chatham House, 1981), p. 33; Keech and Matthews, *The Party's Choice,* p. 202.

60. John C. Greene and Daniel M. Shea, eds., *The State of the Parties,* 3rd Edition (Lanham, Md.: Rowman & Littlefield, 1999), pp. 265, 266.

61. Cited in W. Wayne Shannon, "Evaluating the New Nominating System: Thoughts after 1988 from a Governance Perspective," in *Nominating the President,* Emmett H. Buell, Jr. and Lee Sigelman (Knoxville: University of Tennessee Press, 1991), p. 258.

62. Cited in E. Digby Baltzell, "Blue-Blood Blues," *The New Republic,* April 3, 1989, p. 16.

63. Herman Finer, *The Presidency: Crisis and Regeneration* (Chicago: University of Chicago Press, 1960), p. 281.

64. Arthur Schlesinger Jr., *The Imperial Presidency* (Boston: Houghton Mifflin, 1989), p. 437.

65. Stephen Skowronek, *The Politics Presidents Make: Leadership from John Adams to George Bush* (Cambridge: Belknap Press, 1993), p. 411.

66. Walter Dean Burnham, "The Reagan Heritage," in *The Election of 1988: Reports and Interpretations,* Gerald M. Pomper, et al., (Chatham, N.J.: Chatham House, 1989), p. 1.

67. Alan Binder, "High Clouds, No Storm in Sight," *New York Times,* August 24, 1999, A19.

68. See, for example, Thomas Reeves, *A Question of Character* (New York: Free Press, 1991); Seymour Hersh, *The Dark Side of Camelot* (Boston: Little, Brown, 1997).

69. See, for example, Bob Woodward, *The Agenda: Inside the Clinton White House* (New York: Simon & Schuster, 1994), pp. 25, 70, 86; Elizabeth Drew, *On the Edge: The Clinton Presidency* (New York: Simon & Schuster, 1994), p. 56.

70. David Broder, "A Better Choice of Candidates," *Washington Post,* August 29, 1979, A25. See also David Lebedoff, "The Primary Problem of Primaries: They Produce Jimmy Carters," *Washington Post,* August 19, 1979, E1–E4; Shannon, "Evaluating the New Nominating System," p. 257.

71. See, for example, Nathan Miller, *Star-Spangled Men: America's Ten Worst Presidents* (New York: Scribner, 1998), ch.1.

72. Skowronek, *The Politics Presidents Make,* pp. 380, 381.

73. See Arthur M. Schlesinger Jr., "The Ultimate Approval Rating," *New York Times Magazine,* December 15, 1996, pp. 48, 49.

74. See, for example, Theodore White, *Breach of Faith: The Fall of Richard Nixon* (New York: Atheneum, 1975), p. 65.

75. Schlesinger, "The Ultimate Approval Rating," pp. 48, 49.

76. See, for example, Nelson Polsby, *The Consequences of Party Reform* (New York: Oxford University Press, 1983), ch. 3; James W. Ceaser, *Reforming the Reforms: A Critical Analysis of the Presidential Selection Process* (Cambridge, Mass.: Ballinger, 1982), pp. 108–111.

77. Kelly D. Patterson, *Political Parties and the Maintenance of Liberal Democracy* (New York: Columbia University Press, 1996), p. 93.

78. Jon R. Bond and Richard Fleisher, *The President in the Legislative Arena* (Chicago: University of Chicago Press, 1990), p. 107.

79. See Jeff Fishel, *Presidents & Promises* (Washington, D.C.: Congressional Quarterly Press, 1985), p. 43.

80. See, for example, Norman Ornstein, "The Open Congress Meets the President," in *Both Ends of the Avenue: The Presidency, the Executive Branch, and the Congress in the 1980s,* ed. Anthony King (Washington, D.C.: American Enterprise Institute, 1983), pp. 185–211; Bond and Fleisher, *The President in the Legislative Arena,* p. 102.

Select Bibliography

Abramowitz, Alan I., and Walter Stone. *Nomination Politics: Party Actions and Presidential Choice.* New York: Praeger, 1984.

Abramson, Paul R., John H. Aldrich, and David W. Rhode. *Change and Continuity in the 1992 Election.* Washington, D.C.: CQ Press, 1994.

———. *Change and Continuity in the 1996 Election.* Washington, D.C.: CQ Press, 1998.

Aldrich, John H. *Before the Convention: Strategies and Choices in Presidential Nomination Campaigns.* Chicago: University of Chicago Press, 1980.

Alexander, Herbert, and Anthony Corrado. *Financing the 1992 Election.* Armank, N.Y.: M. E. Sharpe, 1995.

Barber, James David, ed. *Choosing the President.* Englewood Cliffs, N.J.: Prentice-Hall, 1974.

———. *Race for the Presidency: The Media and the Nominating Process.* Englewood Cliffs, N.J.: Prentice-Hall, 1978.

Bartels, Larry M. *Presidential Primaries and the Dynamics of Public Choice.* Princeton, N.J.: Princeton University Press, 1988.

Brams, Steven J. *The Presidential Election Game.* New Haven: Yale University Press, 1978.

Buell, Emmett H., Jr., and Lee Sigelman, eds. *Nominating the President.* Knoxville: University of Tennessee Press, 1991.

Ceaser, James W. *Presidential Selection: Theory and Development.* Princeton, N.J.: Princeton University Press, 1979.

———. *Reforming the Reforms: A Critical Analysis of the Presidential Selection Process.* Cambridge, Mass.: Ballinger, 1982.

———. *Upside Down and Inside Out: The 1992 Election and American Politics.* Lanham, Md.: Rowman & Littlefield, 1993.

Ceaser, James W., and Andrew E. Busch. *Losing to Win: The 1996 Elections and American Politics.* Lanham, Md.: Rowman & Littlefield, 1997.

Chase, James S. *Emergence of the Presidential Nomination Convention 1789–1832.* Urbana: University of Illinois Press, 1973.

Chester, Lewis, Godfrey Hodgson, and Bruce Page. *An American Melodrama: The Presidential Campaign of 1968.* New York: Viking, 1969.

Cook, Rhodes. *Race for the Presidency: Winning the 1988 Nomination.* Washington, D.C.: CQ Press, 1987.

Crotty, William J. *Decision for the Democrats: Reforming the Party Structure.* Baltimore: Johns Hopkins University Press, 1978.
———. *Party Reform.* New York: Longman, 1983.
Crotty, William J., and John S. Jackson, III. *Presidential Primaries and Nominations.* Washington, D.C.: CQ Press, 1985.
David, Paul T., et al. *Proportional Representation in Presidential Nominating Politics.* Charlottesville: University Press of Virginia, 1980.
David, Paul T., Ralph M. Goldman, and Richard C. Bain. *The Politics of National Party Conventions.* Washington, D.C.: The Brookings Institution, 1960.
David, Paul T., , Malcolm Moos, and Ralph M. Goldman. *Presidential Nominating Politics of 1952.* 5 vols. Baltimore: Johns Hopkins University Press, 1954.
Davis, James W. *Presidential Primaries: Road to the White House.* New York: Thomas Y. Crowell, 1967.
———. *National Conventions in an Age of Party Reform.* Westport, Conn.: Greenwood Press, 1983.
———. *U.S. Presidential Primaries and the Caucus-Convention System: A Sourcebook.* Westport, Conn.: Greenwood Press, 1997.
DiClerico, Robert E., and Eric Uslaner. *Few Are Chosen: Problems in Presidential Selection.* New York: McGraw-Hill, 1984.
Foley, John, Dennis A. Britton, and Eugene B. Everett Jr., eds. *Nominating a President.* New York: Praeger, 1980.
Geer, John. *Nominating Presidents.* Westport, Conn.: Greenwood Press, 1989.
Goldwin, Robert A., ed. *Political Parties in the Eighties.* Washington, D.C.: American Enterprise Institute, 1980.
Grassmuck, George, ed. *Before Nomination: Our Primary Problems.* Washington, D.C.: American Enterprise Institute, 1985.
Hadley, Arthur. *The Invisible Primary.* Englewood Cliffs, N.J.: Prentice-Hall, 1976.
Haskell, John. *Fundamentally Flawed: Understanding and Reforming Presidential Primaries.* Lanham, Md.: Rowman & Littlefield, 1996.
Heard, Alexander, and Michael Nelson, eds. *Presidential Selection.* Durham, N.C.: Duke University Press, 1987.
Hirschfield, Robert S. *Selection/Election: A Forum on the American Presidency.* New York: Aldine, 1982.
Jackson, John S., III, and William Crotty. *The Politics of Presidential Selection.* New York: HarperCollins, 1996.
Keech, William, and Donald R. Matthews. *The Party's Choice.* Washington, D.C.: Brookings Institution, 1976.
Keeter, Scott, and Cliff Zukin. *Uninformed Choice: The Failure of the New Nominating System.* New York: Praeger, 1983.
Kirkpatrick, Jeane J. *Dismantling the Parties: Reflections on Party Reform and Party Decomposition.* Washington, D.C.: American Enterprise Institute, 1978.
Lengle, James I. *Representation and Presidential Primaries: The Democratic Party in the Post-Reform Era.* Westport, Conn.: Greenwood Press, 1981.
Lengle, James I., and Byron Shafer, eds. *Presidential Politics: Readings on Nominations and Elections.* New York: St. Martin's Press, 1980.
Loevy, Robert D. *The Flawed Path to the Presidency 1992.* Albany: SUNY Press, 1995.

Maisel, L. Sandy, ed. *The Parties Respond.* 3rd ed. Boulder, Colo.: Westview, 1998.

Marshall, Thomas R. *Presidential Nominations in a Reform Age.* New York: Praeger, 1981.

Mayer, William G. *In Pursuit of the White House 2000: How We Choose Our Presidential Nominees.* New York: Chatham House, 2000.

National Party Conventions 1831–1992. Washington, D.C.: CQ Press, 1995.

Nelson, Michael, ed. *The Elections of 1996.* Washington, D.C.: CQ Press, 1997.

Orren, Gary R., and Nelson W. Polsby, eds. *Media and Momentum: The New Hampshire Primary and Nominating Politics.* Chatham, N.J.: Chatham House, 1987.

Overacker, Louise. *The Presidential Primary.* New York: Macmillan, 1926.

Palmer, Niall A. *The New Hampshire Primary and the American Electoral Process.* Westport, Conn.: Greenwood Press, 1997.

Parris, Judith. *The Convention Problem: Issues in Reform of Presidential Nominating Procedures.* Washington, D.C.: Brookings Institution, 1972.

Patterson, Kelly D. *Political Parties and the Maintenance of Liberal Democracy.* New York: Columbia University Press, 1996.

Patterson, Thomas E. *The Mass Media Election.* New York: Praeger, 1980.

———. *Out of Order.* New York: Random House, 1993.

Pika, Joseph A., and Richard A. Watson. *The Presidential Contest.* 5th ed. Washington, D.C.: CQ Press, 1996.

Polsby, Nelson W. *Consequences of Party Reform.* New York: Oxford University Press, 1983.

Polsby, Nelson W., and Aaron Wildavsky. *Presidential Elections: Strategies and Structures in American Politics.* 9th ed. Chatham, N.J.: Chatham House, 1996.

Pomper, Gerald M. *Nominating the President: The Politics of Convention Choice.* New York: W. W. Norton, 1966.

———. *The Decline of American Political Parties 1952–1996.* Cambridge, Mass.: Harvard University Press, 1998.

———, ed. *The Election of 1992.* Chatham, N.J.: Chatham House, 1993.

Ranney, Austin. *Participation in American Presidential Nominations 1976.* Washington, D.C.: American Enterprise Institute, 1977.

Reichley, A. James, ed. *Elections American Style.* Washington, D.C.: Brookings Institution, 1987.

Reiter, Howard L. *Selecting the President: The Nominating Process in Transition.* Philadelphia: University of Pennsylvania Press, 1985.

Rose, Gary L., ed. *Controversial Issues in Presidential Selection.* 2nd ed. Albany: SUNY Press, 1994.

Sanford, Terry. *A Danger of Democracy: The Presidential Nominating Process.* Boulder, Colo.: Westview, 1981.

Shafer, Byron E. *Quiet Revolution: The Struggle for the Democratic Party and the Shaping of the Post-Reform Politics.* New York: Russell Sage Foundation, 1983.

———. *Bifurcated Politics: Evolution and Reform in the National Party Convention.* Cambridge, Mass.: Harvard University Press, 1988.

Taylor, Paul. *See How They Run: Electing a President in the Age of Mediacracy.* New York: Knopf, 1990.

Thompson, Kenneth W., ed. *The Presidential Nominating Process: Broadening and Narrowing the Debate.* Lanham, Md.: University Press of America, 1983.

Wayne, Stephen J. *The Road to the White House: The Politics of Presidential Elections*
  New York: St. Martin's Press, 1996.
White, Theodore H. *The Making of the President 1960.* New York: Atheneum, 1961.
————. *The Making of the President 1972.* New York: Atheneum, 1973.
————. *America in Search of Itself: The Making of the President 1956–1980.* New
  York: Harper & Row, 1982.
Winebrenner, Hugh. *The Iowa Precinct Caucus: The Making of a Media Event.*
  Ames: Iowa State University, 1987.
Witcover, Jules. *Marathon: The Pursuit of the Presidency 1972–1976.* New York: Vik-
  ing, 1977.

Part Two

Documents

The Guidelines for Delegate Selection

McGovern–Fraser Commission

The Guidelines that we have adopted are designed to eliminate the inequities in the delegate selection process. . . . We view popular participation as the lifeblood of the National Convention system; any compromise with this threatens the future of the Convention.

Since the inception of the Convention system, there has been a trend toward more and more popular participation in the nominating process. First there was the effect of the communications and transportation revolutions of the 19th century. Then there was the introduction of primaries in the early years of this century. In more recent years, Democrats have eliminated the two-thirds rule and racial discrimination. In 1968, the delegates to the Democratic National Convention accelerated this trend with the adoption of the reform resolution and the authorization for the creation of our Commission. In the pages that follow we summarize the Guidelines, which are based on the resolution, discuss the legal status we have to effect the changes our Guidelines require, and present the Guidelines themselves.

SUMMARY OF THE GUIDELINES

The Guidelines are divided into two broad classifications, one in which the Commission *requires* certain action by state Parties, and one in which the Commission *urges* action by the Parties.

The following is a summary of the guidelines the Commission requires state Parties to adopt. "Requires" means that the stated purpose is within the "full, meaningful and timely opportunity" mandate of the 1968 Conven-

Mandate for Reform: A Report of the Commission on Party Structure and Delegate Selection to the Democratic National Committee (Washington, D.C.: Democratic National Committee, 1970), pp. 33–51.

tion, and that the Commission considers the accomplishment of the stated purpose to be the minimum action state Parties must take to meet the requirements of the Call of the 1972 Convention. These Guidelines are meant to apply at all levels of the process by which delegates and alternates are selected.

1. Adopt explicit written Party rules governing delegate selection (A-5).
2. Adopt procedural rules and safeguards for the delegate selection process that would:
   a. forbid proxy voting (B-1).
   b. forbid the use of unit rule and related practices like instructing delegations (B-5).
   c. require a quorum of not less than 40% of all Party committee meetings (B-3).
   d. remove all mandatory assessments of delegates to the National Convention (A-4).
   e. limit mandatory participation fees to no more than $10, and petition requirements to no more than 1% of the standard used to measure Democratic strength (A-4).
   f. ensure that in all but rural areas, Party meetings are held on uniform dates, at uniform times, and in public places of easy access (A-5).
   g. ensure adequate public notice of all Party meetings involved in the delegate selection process (C-1).
3. Seek as broad a base of support for the Party as possible in the following manner:
   a. Add to the party rules and implement the six anti-racial-discrimination standards adopted by the Democratic National Committee (A-1).
   b. Overcome the effects of past discrimination by affirmative steps to encourage representation on the National Convention delegation of minority groups, young people and women in reasonable relationship to their presence in the population of the State (A-1, A-2).
   c. Allow and encourage any Democrat of 18 years of age or older to participate in all Party affairs (A-2).
4. Make, where applicable, the following changes in the delegate selection process:
   a. Select alternates in the same manner as prescribed for the selection of delegates (B-4).
   b. Prohibit the ex-officio designation of delegates to the National Convention (C-2).
   c. Conduct the entire process of delegate selection in a timely manner, i.e., within the calendar year of the Convention (C-4).
   d. In convention systems, select no less than 75% of the total delega-

tion at a level no higher than the congressional district and adopt an apportionment formula which is based on population and/or some standard measure of Democratic strength (B-7).

e. Apportion all delegates to the National Convention not selected at large on a basis of representation which gives equal weight to population and Democratic voting strength based on the previous presidential election (B-7).

f. Designate the procedures by which slates are prepared and challenged (C-6).

g. Select no more than 10% of the delegation by the State committee (C-5).

The following is a summary of the Guidelines the Commission urges state Parties to adopt. "Urges" means that the stated purpose is within the Commission's mandate, that the Commission considers the accomplishment of the stated purpose by the state Parties to be desirable, but that the Commission is not prepared to require such action before the 1972 Convention.

1. Remove all costs and fees involved in the delegate selection process (A-4).

2. Explore ways of easing the financial burden on delegates and alternates and candidates for delegates and alternates (A-4).

3. Assess the burdens imposed on a prospective participant in the delegate selection process by registration laws, customs and practices, and make all feasible efforts to remove or alleviate voter registration laws and practices which prevent the effective participation of Democrats in the delegate selection process. These restrictive laws and practices include annual registration requirements, lengthy residence requirements, literacy tests, short and untimely registration periods, and infrequent enrollment sessions (A-3).

4. Provide for party enrollment that (a) allows non-Democrats to become Party members and (b) provides easy access and frequent opportunity for unaffiliated voters to become Democrats (C-3).

5. Terminate all selection systems which require or permit party committees to select any part of the state delegation (C-5).

6. Adopt procedures which will provide for fair representation of minority views on presidential candidates (B-6). (The Commission has also recommended that the 1972 Convention adopt a rule requiring state Parties to provide representation to minority political views to the highest level of the nominating process. Recognizing the overwhelming importance of this issue, the Commission will make every effort to stimulate systematic public discussion of it now and at the 1972 Democratic National Convention.)

LEGAL STATUS OF THE GUIDELINES

Because the Commission was created by virtue of actions taken at the 1968 Convention, we believe our legal responsibility extends to that body and that body alone. We view ourselves as the agent of that Convention on all matters related to delegate selection. Unless the 1972 Convention chooses to review any steps the Commission has taken, we regard our Guidelines for delegate selection as binding on the states.

We believe that we have been restrained in our exercise of our authority. We have proceeded in much the same manner as any administrative agency. We held hearings, adopted proposed standards, invited comments on those standards and finally adopted our official Guidelines.

Unlike some administrative agencies, however, we have no direct enforcement power. But this does not mean that our Guidelines are merely suggestions for the state Parties.

At the 1964 Convention, the Special Equal Rights Committee was created to "aid the state Democratic parties" in meeting the anti-discrimination requirements of the 1968 Call. After holding a series of hearings, that Committee adopted six basic elements to determine compliance with the 1968 Call. In 1967, Governor Richard Hughes of New Jersey, Chairman of the Committee, attached these elements to a letter he sent to all state chairmen. In the letter, he informed them that in the event of nonconformity with the elements "this Committee will recommend that the Credentials Committee declare the seats to be vacant and fill those seats with a delegation broadly representative of the Democrats of the state."

The Commission on Party Structure and Delegate Selection has the identical legal status and options available to it that the Special Equal Rights Committee had. Although as a matter of policy we plan to work as closely as possible with state Democratic Parties and the Democratic National Committee, we recognize that our obligations to the 1968 Convention may necessitate action similar to that of the Special Equal Rights Committee.

We believe that our Guidelines place no unreasonable demands on state Parties. We did not adopt them with the intention of stimulating credentials challenges in 1972.

In this regard, we did not believe that we should hold state Parties to the same rigid standards if compliance requires a change in state law. Our mandate is to work with state Parties and not with state legislatures—even those with Democratic majorities. Therefore, where compliance would require state legislative or constitutional action, the Commission has relieved state Parties from the obligation of actually accomplishing the required statutory change once "all feasible efforts" have been made. "All feasible efforts" means that the state Party has held hearings, introduced bills, worked for their enactment, and amended its rules in every necessary way short of exposing the Party or its members to legal sanctions.

Regardless of whether conformity is to be achieved by change in state law, or party rule or practice, the Commission believes that state Parties have considerable power at their disposal to democratize their delegate selection process. Therefore the Commission recommends that in the event of any contest or challenge involving an allegation of failure to fulfill the provisions of the following Guidelines, the Credentials Committee of the 1972 Democratic National Convention be guided by the principle that state Parties must assume the burden of ensuring opportunities for full, meaningful and timely participation in the delegate selection process for party members.

"We view popular participation as the lifeblood of the National Convention system; any compromise with this threatens the future of the Convention."

THE OFFICIAL GUIDELINES OF THE COMMISSION

On November 19 and 20, 1969, the Commission, meeting in open session in Washington, D.C., adopted the following Guidelines for delegate selection.

PART I—INTRODUCTION

The following Guidelines for delegate selection represent the Commission's interpretation of the "full, meaningful, and timely" language of its mandate. These Guidelines have been divided into three general categories.

A. Rules or practices which inhibit access to the delegate selection process—items which compromise full and meaningful participation by inhibiting or preventing a Democrat from exercising his influence in the delegate selection process.

B. Rules or practices which dilute the influence of a Democrat in the delegate selection process, after he has exercised all available resources to effect such influence.

C. Rules and practices which have some attributes of both A and B.

A. Rules or practices inhibiting access:

1. Discrimination on the basis of race, color, creed, or national origin.
2. Discrimination on the basis of age or sex.
3. Voter registration.
4. Costs and fees.
5. Existence of Party rules.

B. Rules or practices diluting influence:

1. Proxy voting.
2. Clarity of purpose.
3. Quorum provisions.
4. Selection of alternates; filling of delegate and alternate vacancies.
5. Unit rule.
6. Adequate representation of political minority views.
7. Apportionment.

C. Rules and practices combining attributes of A and B:

1. Adequate public notice.
2. Automatic (ex-officio) delegates.
3. Open and closed processes.
4. Premature delegate selection (timeliness).
5. Committee selection processes.
6. Slate-making.

PART II—THE GUIDELINES

A-1 Discrimination on the basis of race, color, creed, or national origin

The 1964 Democratic National Convention adopted a resolution which conditioned the seating of delegations at future conventions on the assurance that discrimination in any State Party affairs on the grounds of race, color, creed or national origin did not occur. The 1968 Convention adopted the 1964 Convention resolution for inclusion in the Call to the 1972 Convention. In 1966, the Special Equal Rights Committee, which had been created in 1964, adopted six anti-discrimination standards—designated as the "six basic elements"[1]—for the State Parties to meet. These standards were adopted by the Democratic National Committee in January 1968 as its official policy statement.

These actions demonstrate the intention of the Democratic Party to ensure a full opportunity for all minority group members to participate in the delegate selection process. To supplement the requirements of the 1964 and 1968 Conventions, the Commission requires that:

1. State Parties add the six basic elements of the Special Equal Rights Committee to their Party rules and take appropriate steps to secure their implementation;
2. State Parties overcome the effects of past discrimination by affirmative steps to encourage minority group participation, including representation of minority groups on the national convention delegation in rea-

sonable relationship to the groups' presence in the population of the State.[2]

A-2   Discrimination on the basis of age or sex

The Commission believes that discrimination on the grounds of age or sex is inconsistent with full and meaningful opportunity to participate in the delegate selection process. Therefore, the Commission requires State Parties to eliminate all vestiges of discrimination on these grounds. Furthermore, the Commission requires State Parties to overcome the effects of past discrimination by affirmative steps to encourage representation on the national convention delegation of young people—defined as people of not more than thirty nor less than eighteen years of age—and women in reasonable relationship to their presence in the population of the State.[2] Moreover, the Commission requires State Parties to amend their Party rules to allow and encourage any Democrat of eighteen years or more to participate in all party affairs.

When State law controls, the Commission requires State Parties to make all feasible efforts to repeal, amend, or otherwise modify such laws to accomplish the stated purpose.

A-3   Voter registration

The purpose of registration is to add to the legitimacy of the electoral process, not to discourage participation. Democrats do not enjoy an opportunity to participate fully in the delegate selection process in States where restrictive voter registration laws and practices are in force, preventing their effective participation in primaries, caucuses, conventions and other Party affairs. These restrictive laws and practices include annual registration requirements, lengthy residence requirements, literacy tests, short and untimely registration periods, and infrequent enrollment sessions.

The Commission urges each State Party to assess the burdens imposed on a prospective participant in the Party's delegate selection processes by State registration laws, customs and practices, as outlined in the report of the Grass Roots Subcommittee of the Commission on Party Structure and Delegate Selection, and use its good offices to remove or alleviate such barriers to participation.

A-4   Costs and fees; petition requirements

The Commission believes that costs, fees, or assessments and excessive petition requirements made by State law and Party rule or resolutions impose a financial burden on (1) national convention delegates and alternates; (2)

candidates for convention delegates and alternates; and (3) in some cases, participants. Such costs, fees, assessments or excessive petition requirements discouraged full and meaningful opportunity to participate in the delegate selection process.

The Commission urges the State Parties to remove all costs and fees involved in the delegate selection process. The Commission requires State Parties to remove all excessive costs and fees, and to waive all nominal costs and fees when they would impose a financial strain on any Democrat. A cost or fee of more than $10 for all stages of the delegate selection process is deemed excessive. The Commission requires State Parties to remove all mandatory assessments of delegates and alternates.

The Commission requires State Parties to remove excessive petition requirements for convention delegate candidates of presidential candidates. Any petition requirement, which calls for a number of signatures in excess of 1% of the standard used for measuring Democratic strength, whether such standard be based on the number of Democratic votes cast for a specific office in a previous election or Party enrollment figures, is deemed excessive.

When State law controls any of these matters, the Commission requires State Parties to make all feasible efforts to repeal, amend or otherwise modify such laws to accomplish the stated purpose.

This provision, however, does not change the burden of expenses borne by individuals who campaign for and/or serve as delegates and alternates. Therefore, the Commission urges State Parties to explore ways of easing the financial burden on delegates and alternates and candidates for delegate and alternate.

A-5   Existence of Party rules

In order for rank-and-file Democrats to have a full and meaningful opportunity to participate in the delegate selection process, they must have access to the substantive and procedural rules which govern the process. In some States the process is not regulated by law or rule, but by resolution of the State Committee and by tradition. In other States, the rules exist, but generally are inaccessible. In still others, rules and laws regulate only the formal aspects of the selection process (e.g., date and place of the State convention) and leave to Party resolution or tradition the more substantive matters (e.g., intrastate apportionment of votes; rotation of alternates; nomination of delegates).

The Commission believes that any of these arrangements is inconsistent with the spirit of the Call in that they permit excessive discretion on the part of Party officials, which may be used to deny or limit full and meaningful opportunity to participate. Therefore, the Commission requires State Parties to adopt and make available readily accessible statewide Party rules and statutes which prescribe the State's delegate selection process with sufficient details and clarity. When relevant to the State's delegate selection process, explicit written Party rules and procedural rules should include clear provisions for: (1) the apportionment of delegates and votes within the State; (2) the allocation of fractional votes, if any; (3) the selection and responsibilities of convention committees; (4) the nomination of delegates and alternates; (5) the succession of alternates to delegate status and the filling of vacancies; (6) credentials challenges; (7) minority reports.

Furthermore, the Commission requires State Parties to adopt rules which will facilitate maximum participation among interested Democrats in the processes by which National Convention delegates are selected. Among other things, these rules should provide for dates, times, and public places which would be most likely to encourage interested Democrats to attend all meetings involved in the delegate selection process.

The Commission requires State Parties to adopt explicit written Party rules which provide for uniform times and dates of all meetings involved in the delegate selection process. These meetings and events include caucuses, conventions, committee meetings, primaries, filing deadlines, and Party enrollment periods. Rules regarding time and date should be uniform in two senses. First, each stage of the delegate selection process should occur at a uniform time and date throughout the State. Second, the time and date should be uniform from year to year. The Commission recognizes that in many parts of rural America it may be an undue burden to maintain complete uniformity, and therefore exempts rural areas from this provision so long as the time and date are publicized in advance of the meeting and are uniform within the geographic area.

B-1   Proxy voting

When a Democrat cannot, or chooses not to, attend a meeting related to the delegate selection process, many States allow that person to authorize another to act in his name. This practice—called proxy voting—has been a significant source of real or felt abuse of fair procedure in the delegate selection process.

The Commission believes that any situation in which one person is given the authority to act in the name of the absent Democrat, on any issue before the meeting, gives such person an unjustified advantage in affecting the outcome of the meeting. Such a situation is inconsistent with the spirit of equal participation. Therefore, the Commission requires State Parties to add to their explicit written rules provisions which forbid the use of proxy voting in all procedures involved in the delegate selection process.

B-2   Clarity of purpose

An opportunity for full participation in the delegate selection process is not meaningful unless each Party member can clearly express his preference for candidates for delegates to the National Convention, or for those who will select such delegates. In many States, a Party member who wishes to affect the selection of the delegation must do so by voting for delegates or Party officials who will engage in many activities unrelated to the delegate selection process.

Whenever other Party business is mixed, without differentiation, with the delegate selection process, the Commission requires State Parties to make it clear to voters how they are participating in a process that will nominate their Party's candidate for President. Furthermore, in States which employ a convention or committee system, the Commission requires State Parties to clearly designate the delegate selection procedures as distinct from other Party business.

B-3   Quorum provisions

Most constituted bodies have rules or practices which set percentage or number minimums before they can commence their business. Similarly, Party committees which participate in the selection process may commence business only after it is determined that this quorum exists. In some States, however, the quorum requirement is satisfied when less than 40% of committee members are in attendance.

The Commission believes a full opportunity to participate is satisfied only when a rank-and-file Democrat's representative attends such committee meetings. Recognizing, however, that the setting of high quorum requirements may impede the selection process, the Commission requires State Parties to adopt rules setting quorums at not less than 40% for all party committees involved in the delegate selection process.

B-4   Selection of alternates; filling of delegate and alternate vacancies

The Call to the 1972 Convention requires that alternates be chosen by one of the three methods sanctioned for the selection of delegates—i.e., by primary, convention or committee. In some States, Party rules authorize the delegate himself or the State Chairman to choose his alternate. The Commission requires State Parties to prohibit these practices—and other practices not specifically authorized by the Call—for selecting alternates.

In the matter of vacancies, some States have Party rules which authorize State Chairmen to fill all delegate and alternate vacancies. This practice again involves the selection of delegates or alternates by a process other than primary, convention or committee. The Commission requires State Parties to prohibit such practices and to fill all vacancies by (1) a timely and representative Party committee; or (2) a reconvening of the body which selected the delegate or alternate whose seat is vacant; or (3) the delegation itself, acting as a committee.

When State law controls, the Commission requires State Parties to make all feasible efforts to repeal, amend or otherwise modify such laws to accomplish the stated purposes.

B-5   Unit rule

In 1968, many States used the unit rule at various stages in the processes by which delegates were selected to the National Convention. The 1968 Convention defined unit rule,[3] did not enforce the unit rule on any delegate in 1968, and added language to the 1972 Call requiring that "the unit rule not be used in any stage of the delegate selection process." In light of the Convention action, the Commission requires State Parties to add to their explicit written rules provisions which forbid the use of the unit rule or the practice of instructing delegates to vote against their stated preferences at any stage of the delegate selection process.[4]

B-6   Adequate representation of minority views on presidential candidates at each stage in the delegate selection process

The Commission believes that a full and meaningful opportunity to participate in the delegate selection process is precluded unless the presidential preference of each Democrat is fairly represented at all levels of the process. Therefore, the Commission urges each State Party to adopt procedures which will provide fair representation of minority views on presidential candidates and recommends that the 1972 Convention adopt a rule requiring State Parties to provide for the representation of minority views to the highest level of the nominating process.

The Commission believes that there are at least two different methods by which a State Party can provide for such representation. First, in at-large elections it can divide delegate votes among presidential candidates in proportion to their demonstrated strength. Second, it can choose delegates from fairly apportioned districts no larger than congressional districts.

The Commission recognizes that there may be other methods to provide for fair representation of minority views. Therefore, the Commission will make every effort to stimulate public discussion of the issue of representation of minority views on presidential candidates between now and the 1972 Democratic National Convention.

B-7 Apportionment

The Commission believes that the manner in which votes and delegates are apportioned within each State has a direct bearing on the nature of participation. If the apportionment formula is not based on Democratic strength and/or population the opportunity for some voters to participate in the delegate selection process will not be equal to the opportunity of others. Such a situation is inconsistent with a full and meaningful opportunity to participate.

Therefore, the Commission requires State Parties which apportion their delegation to the National Convention to apportion on a basis of representation which fairly reflects the population and Democratic strength within the State. The apportionment is to be based on a formula giving equal weight to total population and to the Democratic vote in the previous presidential election.

The Commission requires State Parties with convention systems to select at least 75% of their delegations to the National Convention at congressional district or smaller unit levels.

In convention or committee systems, the Commission requires State Parties to adopt an apportionment formula for each body actually selecting delegates to State, district and county conventions which is based upon population and/or some measure of Democratic strength. Democratic strength may be measured by the Democratic vote in the preceding presidential, senatorial, congressional or gubernatorial election, and/or by party enrollment figures.

When State law controls, the Commission requires State Parties to make all feasible efforts to repeal, amend or otherwise modify such laws to accomplish the stated purpose.

C-1 Adequate public notice

The Call to the 1968 convention required State Parties to assure voters an opportunity to "participate fully" in party affairs. The Special Equal Rights Committee interpreted this opportunity to include adequate public notice. The Committee listed several elements—including publicizing of the time, places and rules for the conduct of all public meetings of the Democratic Party and holding such meetings in easily accessible places—which comprise adequate public notice. These elements were adopted by the Democratic National Committee in January 1968 as its official policy statement and are binding on the State Parties.

Furthermore, the Commission requires State Parties to circulate a concise and public statement in advance of the election itself of the relationship between the party business being voted upon and the delegate selection process.

In addition to supplying the information indicated above, the Commission believes that adequate public notice includes information on the ballot as to the presidential preference of (1) candidates or slates for delegate or (2) in the States which select or nominate a portion of the delegates by committees, candidates or slates for such committees.

Accordingly, the Commission requires State Parties to give every candidate for delegate (and candidate for committee, where appropriate) the opportunity to state his presidential preferences on the ballot at each stage of the delegate selection process. The Commission requires the State Parties to add the word "uncommitted" or like term on the ballot next to the name of every candidate for delegate who does not wish to express a presidential preference.

When State law controls, the Commission requires the State Parties to make all feasible efforts to repeal, amend or otherwise modify such laws to accomplish the stated purposes.

C-2 Automatic (ex-officio) delegates (see also C-4)

In some States, certain public or Party officeholders are delegates to county, State and National Conventions by virtue of their official position. The Commission believes that State laws, Party rules and Party resolutions which so provide are inconsistent with the Call to the 1972 Convention for three reasons:

1. The Call requires all delegates to be chosen by primary, convention or committee procedures. Achieving delegate status by virtue of public or Party office is not one of the methods sanctioned by the 1968 Convention.
2. The Call requires all delegates to be chosen by a process which begins within the calendar year of the Convention. Ex-officio delegates usually were elected (or appointed) to their positions before the calendar year of the Convention.
3. The Call requires all delegates to be chosen by a process in which all Democrats have a full and meaningful opportunity to participate. Delegate selection by a process in which certain places on the delegation are not open to competition among Democrats is inconsistent with a full and meaningful opportunity to participate.

Accordingly, the Commission requires State Parties to repeal Party rules or resolutions which provide for ex-officio delegates. When State law controls, the Commission requires State Parties to make all feasible efforts to repeal, amend or otherwise modify such laws to accomplish the stated purpose.

C-3   Open and closed processes

The Commission believes that Party membership, and hence opportunity to participate in the delegate selection process, must be open to all persons who wish to be Democrats and who are not already members of another political party; conversely, a full opportunity for all Democrats to participate is diluted if members of other political parties are allowed to participate in the selection of delegates to the Democratic National Convention.

The Commission urges State Parties to provide for party enrollment that (1) allows non-Democrats to become Party members, and (2) provides easy access and frequent opportunity for unaffiliated voters to become Democrats.

C-4   Premature delegate selection (timeliness)

The 1968 Convention adopted language adding to the Call to the 1972 Convention the requirement that the delegate selection process must begin within the calendar year of the Convention. In many States, Governors, State Chairmen, State, district and county committees who are chosen before the calendar year of the Convention, select—or choose agents to select—the delegates. These practices are inconsistent with the Call.

The Commission believes that the 1968 Convention intended to prohibit any untimely procedures which have any direct bearing on the processes by which National Convention delegates are selected. The process by which delegates are nominated is such a procedure. Therefore, the Commission requires State Parties to prohibit any practices by which officials elected or appointed before the calendar year choose nominating committees or propose or endorse a slate of delegates—even when the possibility for a challenge to such slate or committee is provided.

When State law controls, the Commission requires State Parties to make all feasible efforts to repeal, amend, or modify such laws to accomplish the stated purposes.

C-5   Committee selection processes

The 1968 Convention indicated no preference between primary, convention, and committee systems for choosing delegates. The Commission believes, however, that committee systems by virtue of their indirect relationship to the delegate selection process, offer fewer guarantees for a full and meaningful opportunity to participate than other systems.

The Commission is aware that it has no authority to eliminate committee systems in their entirety. However, the Commission can and does require State Parties which elect delegates in this manner to make it clear to voters at the time the Party committee is elected or appointed that one of its functions will be the selection of National Convention delegates.

Believing, however, that such selection system is undesirable even when adequate public notice is given, the Commission requires State Parties to limit the National Convention delegation chosen by committee procedures to not more than 10 percent of the total number of delegates and alternates.

Since even this obligation will not ensure an opportunity for full and meaningful participation, the Commission recommends that State Parties repeal rules or resolutions which require or permit Party committees to select any part of the State's delegation to the National Convention. When State law controls, the Commission recommends that State Parties make all feasible efforts to repeal, amend, or otherwise modify such laws to accomplish the stated purpose.

C-6   Slate-making

In mandating a full and meaningful opportunity to participate in the delegate selection process, the 1968 Convention meant to prohibit any practice in the process of selection which made it difficult for Democrats to participate. Since the process by which individuals are nominated for delegate positions and slates of potential delegates are formed is an integral and crucial part of the process by which delegates are actually selected, the Commission requires State Parties to extend to the nominating process all guarantees of full and meaningful opportunity to participate in the delegate selection process. When State law controls, the Commission requires State Parties to make all feasible efforts to repeal, amend or otherwise modify such laws to accomplish the stated purpose.

Furthermore, whenever slates are presented to caucuses, meetings, conventions, committees, or to voters in a primary, the Commission requires State Parties to adopt procedures which assure that:

1. The bodies making up the slates have been elected, assembled, or appointed for the slate-making task with adequate public notice that they would perform such task;
2. Those persons making up each slate have adopted procedures that will facilitate widespread participation in the slate-making process, with the proviso that any slate presented in the name of a presidential candidate in a primary State be assembled with due consultation with the presidential candidate or his representative.
3. Adequate procedural safeguards are provided to assure that the right to challenge the presented slate is more than perfunctory and places no undue burden on the challengers.

When State law controls, the Commission requires State Parties to make all feasible efforts to repeal, amend or otherwise modify such laws to accomplish the stated purpose.

NOTES

1. *Six basic elements, adopted by the Democratic National Committee as official policy statement, January 1968:*

    1. All public meetings at all levels of the Democratic Party in each State should be open to all members of the Democratic Party regardless of race, color, creed, or national origin.
    2. No test for membership in, nor any oaths of loyalty to, the Democratic Party in any State should be required or used which has the effect of requiring prospective or current members of the Democratic Party to acquiesce in, condone or support discrimination on the grounds of race, color, creed, or national origin.
    3. The time and place for all public meetings of the Democratic Party on all levels should be publicized fully and in such a manner as to assure timely notice to all interested persons. Such meetings must be held in places accessible to all Party members and large enough to accommodate all interested persons.
    4. The Democratic Party, on all levels, should support the broadest possible registration without discrimination on grounds of race, color, creed or national origin.
    5. The Democratic Party in each State should publicize fully and in such manner as to assure notice to all interested parties a full description of the legal and practical procedures for selection of Democratic Party Officers and representatives on all levels. Publication of these procedures should be done in such fashion that all prospective and current members of each State Democratic Party will be fully and adequately informed of the pertinent procedures in time to participate in each selection procedure at all levels of the Democratic Party organization.
    6. The Democratic Party in each State should publicize fully and in such manner as to assure notice to all interested parties a complete description of the legal and practical qualifications for all officers and representatives of the State Democratic Party. Such publication should be done in timely fashion so that all prospective candidates or applicants for any elected or appointed position within each State Democratic Party will have full and adequate opportunity to compete for office.

2. It is the understanding of the Commission that this is not to be accomplished by the mandatory imposition of quotas.

3. Unit Rule. "This Convention will not enforce upon any delegate with respect to voting on any question or issue before the Convention any duty or obligation which said delegate would consider to violate his individual conscience. As to any legal, moral or ethical obligation arising from a unit vote or rule imposed either by State law by a State convention or State committee or primary election of any nature, or by a vote of a State delegation, the Convention will look to each individual delegate to determine for himself the extent of such obligation if any."

4. It is the understanding of the Commission that the prohibition on instructed delegates applies to favorite-son candidates as well.

Part Three

Readings

A Proposal for a National Presidential Primary

Senator Estes Kefauver

Introduction of the presidential primary in various States in the early years of this century was designed to put the presidential nominations more directly into the hands of the people. First adopted by Wisconsin in 1905, this institution was used in 12 States in 1912, in 20 States in 1916, 23 States in 1924, 17 States in 1948, and in 16 States and the District of Columbia in 1960.

In his book, *American Parties and Elections* (1939), Mr. E. M. Sait said:

> The presidential primary represented an attempt to short-circuit an elaborate system of wiring and to deliver the full load of the current—the full force of the popular will—without the fatal leakages that had occurred along the old defective lines of transmission. It was intended to leave the national convention as little discretion in nominating the presidential candidate as the electoral college has in electing him (p. 547).

Forty years ago, President Wilson wrote that:

> there ought never to be another presidential nominating convention. . . . The nominations should be made directly by the people at the polls.

In his first annual message to Congress in December 1913, Wilson formally proposed the establishment of a national presidential primary and the

---

Estes Kefauver served as U.S. Senator from Arkansas (1949–1963). He was an unsuccessful candidate for the Democratic Party presidential nomination in 1952 and received his party's vice presidential nomination in 1956.

From *Hearings Before the Subcommittee on Constitutional Amendments* of the Committee on the Judiciary, United States Senate, 87th Congress, 1st Session. Part I, pp. 268–275.

retention of the convention only for declaring the results of the primary and
formulating the party platform.

LIMITATIONS OF PRESENT STATE PRIMARIES

While the presidential primary is a more direct and democratic method of
nominating presidential candidates than the convention system, it has some
serious limitations at present, the principal one being that it has been
adopted by so few States. It is limited, therefore, by the extent of its use. In
less than one-third of the States last year did the voters have a choice in the
selection of delegates to the national conventions.

Of these 16 States, only 3—California, Ohio, and Oregon—require, effectively, that delegates be pledged to a certain candidate. Indiana's delegates are
pledged for the first ballot only. Five States—New Hampshire, Wisconsin,
Massachusetts, Florida, and South Dakota—provide that delegates may be
pledged to specific candidates or may indicate a preference, but neither is
mandatory.

Seven other States—Florida, Nebraska, Illinois, New Jersey, Pennsylvania,
Maryland, and West Virginia—and the District of Columbia provide merely
for the election of unpledged delegates. In 34 States the voters have no votes
in the selection of their delegates to the national convention. (Alabama and
Arkansas have laws permitting primaries, but they usually are not held).

Thus the presidential primary device, since it is a State and not a national
primary system, lacks uniformity in the nature of its methods for carrying
out the popular will. Some State primary laws are devoted solely to electing
delegates to national conventions. Others provide for both a presidential
preference vote and for the election of delegates.

The laws also vary as to whether the delegates are pledged or unpledged
and in the form of instructions to the delegates. No two laws are identical.

In practice, moreover, the presidential primary system, as it is now operated on a State basis, has disclosed certain weaknesses. The proportion of the
delegates to the conventions by primary States is too small to be decisive
unless almost all of them support the same candidate, and even then the expressed will of the people may be frustrated by the maneuvering in the convention.

Furthermore, not all the primary States afford an opportunity to choose
among all leading contenders for the nominations. Some aspirants prefer to
keep their hats out of the ring until at least the first few primaries have been
held. Many candidates, out of courtesy or prudence, refrain from entering
the primary of a State with a strong "favorite son."

Obviously, the results of a primary where voters have no chance to express themselves on all the leading candidates, except through write-in votes,

do not necessarily measure sentiment within the State or afford clear guidance to the conventions.

When all candidates do enter a primary under the present situation, its result may have an exaggerated psychological effect. We have seen how the eyes of the Nation and the concentrated efforts of the candidates turn to the primary of one particular State where all the leading contestants have entered.

The winner, as a practical matter, often delivers the deathblow to his opponents merely because of the results in that State. One State's voters, in effect, may have made the choice for the voters in all States. Thus, scattered State primaries, with the leading candidates entered in only a few, may actually lead us away from nomination of the true choice of the voters of the entire country. The primary victory which paved the way to nomination may have been determined by the candidates' views on local issues which are of little importance in other States or by voter appeal in one State which would have worked oppositely in another.

Election of delegates and preferential voting by congressional districts also work to confuse the picture. A classic example was the election by an Illinois district in 1920 of an avowed supporter of Senator Hiram Johnson as its delegate to the Republican convention, while Gen. Leonard Wood was winning the district's presidential preference vote, and Gov. Frank Lowden was winning the preference vote of the State as a whole.

In some States, moreover, delegates at large are chosen by the party organizations. Hence, if the State machine does not favor the candidate who wins the State's preference vote and the largest number of district delegates, it is in a position to send delegates to the convention.

Another feature which may tend to weaken the present presidential primary system as a method of popular control over nominations is the variation of provisions in State laws with regard to the consent of the candidates whose names, or those of their pledged delegates, appear in the ballot. Most State laws require specific consent by candidates.

But a name may appear without consent in Oregon if enough voters sign petitions, and the unwilling entry is left to file an affidavit that he is not a candidate. In Indiana, specific consent is not required, but a non-Communist affidavit must be filed by any person for whom a petition is filed. The unwilling candidate's only means of staying off the ballot is one that he is not likely to want to use—failure to file a non-Communsit affidavit.

Popular control of the nominating process is also affected by the so-called favorite-son game. One feature of this game is the tendency to bring forth favorite sons from the different States who are not really serious contenders for the presidential nomination, but are proposed sometimes merely to honor a leading citizen or politician, or more often with the deliberate purpose of reducing the support of some more important candidate, or of holding large blocs of votes which will produce a deadlock and can later be used in the convention for trading purposes.

Another feature of the favorite-son game is the practice of field against the favorite in which all the favorite sons pool their strength in the convention against one outstanding candidate, on the hope that he will be defeated and the lightning will strike one of them. In view of this practice, writes Prof. Clarence Berdahl:

> It is nothing short of amazing that the people's choice ever wins, and, in fact, leading statesmen are discouraged from entering the primaries at all ("Presidential Selection and Democratic Government," *Journal of Politics*, 1949).

In view of all these limitations of the existing convention and primary systems, there is no assurance that the convention results reflect the real desires of the party rank and file and present primaries contribute little toward this assurance. As Berdahl concluded in 1949:

> It is only possible to assert that there is in the presidential primary, especially with some method of instructions, an opportunity for popular participation and influence in respect to presidential nominations that can easily be developed more fully if such development is desired.

ADVANTAGES OF PRIMARIES

In the light of our historical development toward the democratization of the present presidential nominating and election process, and of these weaknesses of the present presidential primary system, I suggest that the time has come to take the next step toward extending popular control of presidential nominations.

The primary method of nomination works well in selecting Governors and Members of Congress in many States. It should be extended to the choice of candidates for President and Vice President and thus continue the evolution toward more democratic methods of choosing our presidential and vice-presidential candidates. The more the people have a chance to speak their minds, the closer we get to grassroots opinions and desires, the better our democracy works.

Presidential primary elections in all the States would require candidates to discuss the issues publicly. Such public debate will help to inform and enlighten public opinion via press, radio, and television, and it would pave the way for broadening and strengthening the democratic process.

It will also result, I believe, in better government, and government more responsible to the people. A candidate for President who has been nominated by the people instead of the conventions will be, if elected, more responsive to the will of the people and more obligated to the people than to politicians.

Experience shows that presidential primaries arouse public interest and stimulate discussions of public issues, as well as of the character, convictions, and abilities of those who aspire to the highest offices in the land. They also increase the participation of eligible voters in presidential elections and overcome the apathy induced by the feeling that the people have little real choice in the selection of their candidates for President and Vice President.

In this period of struggle between the democracies and the dictatorships, the method of choosing the men who lead our Nation should leave no room for doubt, at home or abroad, that our leaders have been elected after the fullest possible freedom of choice by our people. The archaic convention system does not necessarily register the preferences of the people.

Television has revealed to the American people the inefficient and undemocratic aspects of the convention system. Its weaknesses and defects have been observed at home and abroad. Public opinion polls show that the people overwhelmingly favor abolition of the convention system and substitution of primary elections.

PROPOSED REFORMS

I feel that the details of primary elections should not be given inflexibility by inclusion in a constitutional amendment. However, Congress cannot require nomination by primaries by legislation without an enabling constitutional amendment because the Constitution leaves to the States the manner of appointment of electors in the electoral college, which constitutionally is still the body which selects the President and Vice President.

I believe, too, that the proposal for a national presidential primary has a greater chance for success if we advance it first as a general principle, then work out the details after the reform has been approved by constitutional referendum. For this reason I purposely kept my resolution simple and non-specific as to details.

In the January 31, 1953, issue of *Collier's* magazine, I wrote an article which included a pattern for nationwide presidential primaries and nominating conventions. I still believe that its basic outlines are sound, and I will work for adoption of a bill along its general lines if the idea is adopted as a constitutional amendment. The plan which I then suggested, with a discussion of each step, is as follows:

Step 1: There shall be a primary in every State, provided for by Federal law, to determine the popular choice of the people for President. In each primary, delegates shall be elected to cast their votes at a streamlined national convention for the choice of their State's voters.

These delegates, presumably, will also approve the platform upon which the party's nominees will campaign. This will help to insure that the candidate and platform are fully compatible with each other and that both represent the choice of the voters in the party.

Discussion: There have been presidential primaries in various States since Wisconsin passed the first such State law in 1903. Currently, 18 States have primary laws of one sort or another. The laws, however, are not uniform, and in some States are not even binding on the delegates; the lack of uniformity, plus the fact that most of the States do not have primaries, leads to a helter-skelter pattern which lessens the significance of primaries. With a uniform and binding law applicable to every State, presidential primaries would become meaningful.

Step 2: No candidate shall be placed on the ballot in any State primary without his consent, and he must file a qualifying petition signed by not less than 1 percent of the total number of voters who voted for the presidential candidate of his party in the last election.

Discussion: This provision would make it necessary for a man to be a willing candidate and to work for his nomination. It follows the wholesome example of President Kennedy in 1960, who openly declared his candidacy and gave opposing candidates and the voters every possible chance for expression in primary elections. I believe it is a good principle, and a democratic one, for "the man to seek the job"—particularly under the proposed new system where the voters really would have something to say about selection of candidates. It also will eliminate many of the nonserious candidates—favorite sons and others.

Step 3: A uniform nationwide system of choosing delegates, based, in part at least, on the vote of the political party of each State in the last previous presidential election. There should be provisions to limit the number of delegates so as to avoid the present unwieldy size of national conventions, and there shall be no split votes—such as one-half and one-third votes.

Discussion: It would be politically healthy to peg a State's delegates to the total votes mustered by the party in the last election. This would encourage all segments of the party to get out the vote in every election. More importantly, it will apply the principle of democratic representation within the party according to its effective membership—the number of voters.

I suggest that, instead of the present 1,400-odd votes at a convention, with some of them split between 2 or 3 persons, the total be limited to no more than 600, with no split votes. It is impossible to conduct an orderly convention with almost 3,000 delegates (counting the split votes)—not to mention their alternates—milling about.

Step 4: Delegates shall be firmly pledged to cast their votes on a proportional basis geared to the State vote received by the candidate. As a simple illustration, if a State has 10 delegates and candidate A receives approximately 60 percent of the vote, he will receive 6 votes at a convention. (To avoid undesirable fractional ballots, machinery can be set up where the division of delegates is calculated by round numbers, rather than by exact fractions.)

The delegates will continue to vote for the candidate to whom they are pledged as long as he receives as many as 10 percent of the total vote cast at the convention (with certain provisions in case of deadlock).

Discussion: I have given thought to the alternate possibility of having the candidate who receives a plurality of the State vote capture all the State delegates. I believe, however, that proportional division is fairer, and would reflect the wishes of the voters more accurately. Such a division is more in line with my belief that the electoral college vote should be divided proportionately, rather than letting the candidate who gets the most popular votes in a State take all of the State's electoral votes.

Another possible alternative, which might be considered as an interim measure pending reform of the electoral college machinery, would be a Federal primary law patterned after the excellent Wisconsin State law. In Wisconsin, the candidate receiving the largest statewide vote wins a certain number of delegates running as the State delegates at large, while winners in various congressional districts get the votes of delegates for those districts.

As a means of breaking an early deadlock, a candidate should be given discretionary authority to release his delegates when he feels he cannot win. The law should be written to indicate strongly that the delegates, once released, are free agents, at liberty to exercise their best judgment as to preference among the remaining eligible candidates; the practice of trading delegates to accomplish private political deals should be discouraged.

The Wisconsin primary law is again a good example. It binds a pledged delegate to vote for his candidate until he is released or the candidate receives less than 10 percent of the total vote on any ballot. The delegate is then free to exercise his own judgment.

Step 5: Nomination for President shall be by a simple majority of the total number of votes cast by delegates at the convention. If no candidate has a majority, and has not released his delegates, after 10 ballots the delegates shall be considered free of their obligation to vote for the winner of their State primary, but must vote for one of the candidates receiving the top three total number of votes in the national primary.

Discussion: This step provides a key which makes the proposed system practical. In combination with step 4, it would mitigate the nuisance value of any surviving favorite son, who could not hope to hang on for 10 ballots, but would try to trade delegates for favors.

The provision for picking the presidential nominee from the aspirants who placed first, second, and third in the nationwide primary popular vote is a means of respecting the will of the voters. It also has constitutional precedent, for the 12th amendment provides that, in the case of a deadlock in the electoral college, the House of Representatives shall select a President from among the top three candidates.

Step 6: Finally, after the presidential nominee is chosen, the vice-presidential nominee shall be chosen by a vote of the delegates from the three candidates who polled the next highest number of votes in the nationwide primaries.

Discussion: This is the procedure followed by the Democratic convention in 1956 when I was nominated for Vice President. It respects the wishes of the electorate and insures that the office of Vice President is not an object of political barter.

It would mean that the Vice President post would go to a man sufficiently interested in public service to get out and work for his nomination in a primary, and that the post would be filled by a man whom the people know, and who was of sufficient stature to have placed at least fourth in the national presidential primary.

It can be said of too few vice-presidential nominees that they were the choice of the people. Under the system I propose, there would be an opportunity for any political skeletons hiding in the closets of the eventual presidential and vice-presidential candidates to be brought into the open—before, not after, the nomination.

We must remember that a Vice President always is a "serious candidate" for President, for seven times in our history Presidents have died in office. The office of Vice President always should be filled by mature, capable individuals of whom the voters have full knowledge.

Senate Joint Resolution 9, introduced by Senator Smathers of Florida, combines with presidential primaries and electoral college reform a provision that if a Vice President succeeds to the Presidency by reason of death there shall be a special presidential election at the next general election to choose a new President. This procedure, in my opinion, would be cumbersome. The system by which one of the top four choices of the victorious party would become Vice President would eliminate the necessity for such a special election.

Another healthy reform desired by many evolves naturally from this plan. It is a shorter general election campaign period for the men finally chosen by the major parties as presidential nominees. The party candidates would already have fought out the primaries, which would be held simultaneously throughout the country on a fixed date in August.

The national convention then could be held in September. Assuming that the successful candidates would take the usual amount of time to map out their campaign, the actual campaigning could be limited pretty much to the month of October. That plan would be good life insurance for our Chief Executive.

I would like to see all campaigning elevated to a less strenuous, more intellectual level, with less wear and tear on the candidates. I have never seen any sense in practically killing off our Presidents before we select them, and I am sure that the American people do not want that.

In conclusion, the long-run trend has been toward the gradual democratization of our electoral system. Discretionary voting in the electoral college was early removed. Property qualifications for voting disappeared more than a century ago. The 14th and 15th amendments were adopted after the War Between the States. The direct election of Senators and woman suffrage continued the evolution in this direction. Enfranchisement of the District of Columbia this year is another milestone. It remains now to democratize our methods of nominating and electing the President and Vice President.

The Case for a National Pre-primary Convention Plan

Thomas Cronin and Robert Loevy

Our presidential nominating process has changed dramatically since the 1960s when John F. Kennedy entered just four contested state primaries. Once shaped mainly by state and national party leaders, it is increasingly shaped by single-interest groups and the media.

The formal nominating process begins with the Iowa caucus in January of an election year and lumbers through more state caucuses and conventions and thirty-six primary elections before candidates are finally selected at national party conventions in July and August.

Nobody, with the possible exception of Ronald Reagan, seems happy with the present nominating system—especially the patchworky maze of presidential primaries. The process strains patience and, critics say, eliminates good candidates. The current primary system plainly favors well-heeled out-of-office individuals who can devote their full attention to selected early state nominating battles. Thus Carter in 1976, and Reagan in 1980, could spend up to a hundred days in Iowa, New Hampshire, and Florida, while officeholders such as Udall, Baker, Anderson, Kennedy, and the sitting presidents had to remain on their jobs.

Our present nominating process has become a televised horse race focusing more on media appeal than on the competing ideas, programs, or character of the candidates. More voters, to be sure, take part in primary elections than in caucuses and conventions. But what about the *quality* of that participation? Primary voters often know little about the many candidates listed

Thomas Cronin is a political scientist and president of Whitman College. Robert Loevy is a professor of political science at Colorado College.

From *Public Opinion* ([December/January] 1983). Reprinted with the permission of the American Enterprise Institute for Public Policy Research.

on the ballot. Popularity polls, slick spot ads, and television coverage of the early primaries offer episodes and spectacles, and the average citizen is hard pressed to separate significance from entertainment.

MOMENTUM FEVER

"Winners"—sometimes with only 20 percent of the vote—in the early small state nomination contests are given undue media coverage. For example, Jimmy Carter's victories in Iowa and New Hampshire in 1976 led to an out-pouring of cover and human interest stories on him.

Voters in New Hampshire and a few other early primaries often virtually get the right to nominate their party's candidate. Candidates who do not do well in these early states get discouraged, and their financial contributors and volunteers desert them. In most presidential years, the nominees of both major parties are decided much too early in the process.

Critics are also concerned, rightly we believe, about the declining importance of the national conventions. Now that nominations are often "sewed up" by early primaries, the national conventions have become *ratifying* rather than *nominating* conventions. Most delegates, bound by various state and party election rules, have little more to do than cast their predetermined required vote, enjoy a round of cocktail parties, pick up local souvenirs, and go home. It is little wonder that the networks are moving away from gavel-to-gavel coverage.

A further complaint is that the current nominating system has diminished the role of party and public officials, and concomitantly increased the role of candidate loyalists and issue activists. Primaries bypass the local party structure by encouraging candidates and their managers to form candidate-loyalist brigades several months before the primaries. Elected officials generally are unwilling to become committed to one candidate or another until well along in the election year and hence they are often excluded from the process. But because most serious candidates for national office hold (or have held) elective office, the views of their peers can be particularly insightful. Because elected officials, especially members of Congress, have some obligation to implement the goals and platform of their party, they should participate in the development of the party positions.

Elected officials plead to be brought back into the system; to be given incentives for involvement; to be given responsibility in selecting candidates and writing the platform. Let us integrate the national presidential party and the congressional party as one working unit where all the various components have some status and voice in the processes and outcomes.

Strengthening the party role in the nominating process does not require that elected or party leaders dominate or control nominations. Rather, it would encourage peer review and ensure that a reasonable number of elected officials are allowed to participate. Political scientist Everett Ladd suggests that the person who successfully "passes muster in a peer review process, if elected, comes into office with contacts and alliances that he needs if he is to govern successfully."

United States Senator Alan Cranston (D-Calif.) raises objections to the present system. He claims that few, if any, of the qualities that bring victory in primaries are the qualities the presidency demands.

> Primaries do not tell us how well a candidate will delegate authority. Nor do they demonstrate his ability to choose the best people for top government posts. . . . Primaries don't tell us how effective a candidate will be in dealing with Congress, nor how capable a candidate will be at moving the national power structure, nor how good an educator of the American public a candidate would really be as president. . . . Primaries do not adequately test courage and wisdom in decision making—yet those are the ultimate tests of a good president.

THE ALTERNATIVE

We are more than a little aware that no procedure is neutral, that any system has various side-effects and unanticipated consequences. Further, we know that no method of nominating presidential candidates guarantees good candidates or good presidents. (The nominating method used in selecting Lincoln also gave us Buchanan. The methods that nominated Eisenhower and Kennedy nominated Richard Nixon as a member of the national ticket on five different occasions.) Plainly, no procedure can substitute for rigorous screening and the exercise of shrewd judgment at every step.

We think there is an intriguing alternative to the present system of nominating presidential candidates. Known as the National Pre-primary Convention Plan, it would reverse the present order of things. It would replace thirty-six individual state primaries with a caucus and convention system in all states, to be followed by a national convention, which in turn would be followed by a national Republican presidential primary and a national Democratic presidential primary to be held on the same day in September.

Although this proposal challenges the prevailing notion that the presidential primary should occur before the convention, there are working precedents at the state level. The proposal is new only when applied at the national level. At the state level, it has been well tested. Colorado, for example, has used this system since 1910 and has found it a good way to retain the strengths of both the party convention and the party primary election.

DELEGATES BOUND AND UNBOUND

A National Pre-primary Convention Plan starts with nationwide party caucuses on the first Monday in May of the presidential year. Any citizen would
be eligible to attend a particular party caucus, but, in order to vote there, he
would have to register at the caucus as a member of that political party. By
national law, those who register in a political party at the precinct caucus
could vote only in that particular party's national primary the following
September.

Party members at the party caucus would be eligible to run for delegate
to the county party convention. Those candidates for delegate who wished
to identify themselves as supporting a particular candidate for president
could do so, and they would be bound to vote for that candidate when they
attended the county convention.

The county conventions would be held on the second Saturday in May.
County convention delegates would elect delegates to the state party conventions, which would be held on the first Saturday in June. The state conventions would elect the state delegations to the national party conventions,
which would be held in July.

Similar to the procedure at the precinct caucuses, candidates for delegate
at the county and congressional district conventions would state their preferences among competing presidential candidates, or state their preferences to
remain uncommitted. Those stating a preference would then be committed
or "bound" only on the first ballot at the national conventions.

We propose, and the National Pre-primary Convention Plan would
readily accommodate, the selection at the state party convention of 25 percent of the state's delegation to the national convention as "unbound" delegates. These persons so designated might be nominated by the state central
committees from available state elected and party leaders who have demonstrated strong commitment to their party. Such officials might include several members of the state's congressional delegation, statewide elected officers such as governor and attorney general, a few big-city mayors, and state
legislators as well as state party leaders. These unbound delegates would
sometimes mirror local and state caucus results. They would have an obligation to exercise their best political judgment, not simply to abide by public
opinion and the temporary wishes of their supporters. Their presence and
their perspective should help make national conventions more deliberative
and more occasions for party renewal than has been the case in recent years.
These officials could also take into consideration late-breaking events or reflect current opinion in July as opposed to the public moods earlier in the
spring.

THE RULES OF THE GAME

States would be prohibited by national law from holding any form of official preconvention presidential primary election. Throughout the entire process, the emphasis would be on selecting party members as delegates.

Voting procedures and other operational details at the party caucus, the county convention, congressional districts, and the state conventions would be left to individual state laws and national political party rules. The structure, organization, and scheduling of the Democratic and Republican national conventions would be the same as they are now, with the exception that both conventions would be held in July instead of one in July and the other in August.

The major task, as always, of the national convention would be to nominate candidates for the national party primary the following September. On the first of two ballots, bound delegates would vote for their declared choice, and unbound delegates could vote for any candidate. After the first ballot, all candidates except the top three finishers would be eliminated. The top three candidates would then run against each other on the second ballot, at which time *all* delegates would be unbound and could vote their preference.

The authors are of two minds about what should happen at this point. One of us believes that only the top two remaining candidates (so long as each receives a minimum of 30 percent from the convention) should be placed on the national primary ballot.

The other one believes that the endorsement threshold should be lowered to 25 percent, with the possibility that three candidates be allowed on the national primary ballot. If three candidates are placed on the primary ballot, a procedure called "approval voting" would come into effect. Under approval voting, voters can vote for as many candidates as they like. Thus if Reagan, Bush, and Baker were on the national Republican primary ballot in September 1984, a moderate Republican might vote for both Baker and Bush, while a conservative Republican might decide to vote for Reagan, or to vote for both Bush and Reagan. Approval voting is, in part, an insurance plan preventing an unrepresentative or least preferred candidate from winning in the three-person race.

Regardless of which formula is used to get two or three candidates in the party's national primary, only those candidates among the top three who received 25 percent of the vote or more on the second ballot would appear on the September primary ballot.

In certain presidential years, a candidate might be so strong at the convention that he would not have to face a national primary election. This would occur when, on the second ballot, neither the second-place nor the third-place candidate had 25 percent of the convention vote (or under our other alternative, when the second of two top finishers had less than 30 percent). Some states which use the Pre-primary Convention Plan also declare that the candidate who receives 70 percent of the state convention automatically receives the party's nomination. This same stipulation should apply at the national level. It would be expected, for instance, that a popular incumbent president with strong support from his own party could avoid the strain of a September primary.

The final duty of the national party convention would be to create a pool of acceptable vice-presidential prospects from which the eventual presidential nominee would make a choice following the national primary in September. All of the candidates who qualify for the second ballot at the convention would automatically be in this vice-presidential pool. The convention could add up to three more vice-presidential candidates. Immediately following the party presidential primary election in September, the winning candidate would select his vice-presidential nominee from the candidates in the pool.

The National Democratic Presidential Primary and the National Republican Presidential Primary would both be held on the same day, the second Tuesday after the first Monday in September (after August vacations and Labor Day weekend).

Any voter who was registered in a particular party by July 1 of the presidential year would be eligible to vote in that party's national presidential primary. The date of July 1 is suggested because it is late enough that those citizens who have had their partisan interests stimulated by the local precinct caucuses and state and county conventions still will be able to register in a particular political party. The goal here is to prevent partisan voters whose party is not having a presidential primary in a particular year from switching their registration in order to vote for the weakest opposition candidate.

If there are, or should be in the future, states that do not provide under state law for voter registration in the two major political parties, the United States Congress should pass any necessary national laws to guarantee that all United States citizens have the right to register in a particular political party and vote in the September presidential primary.

The one candidate who gets the most votes in the September primary would be the party candidate in the November general election. A plurality of votes rather than a majority would be sufficient to declare the winner. In case of a tie, or in case of a close race where large numbers of ballots were contested, or if the winning candidate dies or becomes functionally disabled, the party national committee shall decide the official party candidate for the November election.

As noted above, the first official event following the national primary would be the selection of the vice-presidential candidate by the presidential nominee. Note that the presidential candidate will have considerable latitude in selecting his party running mate. If it appears propitious to select one of his defeated opponents and thereby mend party fences, he is free to do so. If he wishes not to choose a defeated opponent, however, he has three candidates available who have been officially approved by the candidate.

SOME ADVANTAGES OF THE PRE-PRIMARY CONVENTION PLAN

The National Pre-primary Convention Plan is designed to eliminate the more criticized characteristics of the present presidential nominating system and also to provide some positive additions not found in the present system:

- Replacement of the present six-month series of thirty-six individual state primaries by a single national primary election campaign that would last only six to eight weeks
- Increased voter interest (and turnout) generated by a single national party primary election
- Reduction of the media's tendency to concentrate on political "momentum" rather than a candidate's character and issue positions in the early small state primaries
- Elimination of regional advantages for those candidates who are lucky enough to have strong support in early state primaries
- A return to the *nominating* rather than *ratifying* convention
- Re-emphasis on the importance of party membership and influence of party caucuses and conventions
- A strengthening of the average voter's role in the final decision
- Increased incumbent responsibility to his own party
- Increased role for party and elected officials

POSSIBLE OBJECTIONS

No plan is perfect, and there are some possible defects in the National Pre-primary Convention Plan. Here are likely concerns and our discussion of them.

- Having all the local caucuses and state conventions taking place at the same time would make it more difficult for less known and less well-financed candidates to attract attention (and money).

  Our response in favor of the Pre-primary Convention Plan is that the cost of entering state caucuses is significantly, perhaps four times, lower than entering state primaries as a serious candidate. Second, a candidate need do well in only a handful of states to prove his or her abilities and capture at least some national delegates. Since the nomination would not usually be decided on the first ballot, a number of worthy candidates would be able to survive and thus obtain peer review and political scrutiny before the convention makes its final determination.

- Some will contend that the National Pre-primary Convention Plan is too national, too rigid, and too mechanistic. They might add that it diminishes federalism, at least to the extent it tells states when and how they will select delegates.

  Our response is that the presidency is a national office. Further, it is clear that the national parties have both the responsibility and the authority to decide on the procedure for the nomination of a presidential candidate. Finally, this new plan will strengthen the party at the state level, and it treats all states as equals.

- Critics are likely to say that the national primary feature of this new plan will encourage television and media events of the worst possible kind.

  Our plan will actually diminish much of the negative influence of television in the preconvention stage of a campaign. It will require presidential candidates to meet with party and elected local leaders and to build coalitions at the grass-roots level—not just appear in television spot ads.

- Some critics may fear this will diminish the role of minorities and lessen the affirmative action gains of the past decade—especially gains made in the Democratic party.

  We do not think this will be the case. Existing affirmative action rules may just as easily apply. Indeed, the increased turnout at the national primaries should enhance minority participation.

- What about its effect on third or minor parties? Third parties would still have their national conventions, but they would seldom need a national primary. A rule could be devised so that any national party receiving at least 5 percent of the vote in the past presidential election could participate in the national primary arrangements.

- Wouldn't the national primary be an even greater expense to the states? Perhaps. But conducting the national primary in fifty states in the fall as opposed to thirty-six in the spring is not really much different.

Here is a plan, we think, that shortens the formal election season and simplifies it so the average voter can understand its operations. More than the present system, it will test the political coalition-building skills of serious candidates—those skills so needed to win the general election and to govern; allow for sensible participation from all segments of the party; promote revitalized parties that are subject to popular control; facilitate and encourage the best possible candidates, including busy officeholders, to run for the presidency; encourage participatory caucuses and conventions at all levels of our system; and finally, it will go a long way toward rescuing the all but doomed national conventions and help make them more of an occasion for reflective societal leadership.

Approval Voting: A Practical Reform for Multicandidate Elections

Stephen J. Brams

Approval voting is a system in which a voter may choose or approve of as many candidates as desired in a multicandidate election. For example, a voter might vote for just one candidate, or for several candidates if more than one is found acceptable. However, only one vote may be cast for every approved candidate—that is, votes may not be cumulated and several cast for one candidate. The candidate with the most votes wins.

With approval voting, two or more candidates each could receive the votes of more than 50 percent of the voters, though in a large field of candidates such an outcome would probably be unlikely. Even so, the thought that more than one candidate could be supported by a majority of voters does seem strange. So does the idea of giving voters the opportunity to vote for more than one candidate that can produce this result. Yet, approval voting is not only compatible with most constitutions but it also has several advantages over plurality voting, plurality voting with a runoff (if no candidate receives a majority in the first election), and preferential voting (in which voters can rank candidates). Moreover, it is practical: among other things, it can readily be implemented on existing voting machines, and it is more efficient than holding both a plurality and runoff election.

Here are the main arguments for approval voting:

1. *It is best for the voters.* Approval voting allows citizens to do exactly what they do now—vote for their favorite candidate—but, if they have no clear favorite, it also allows them to express this fact by voting for all candidates that they rank highest. In addition, if a favorite seems to have little

Stephen J. Brams is a professor of political science at New York University.

From *National Civic. Review* 68:10 (New York: National Municipal League, November 1979). Reprinted by permission.

chance of winning, the voter can still cast a ballot for that candidate without worrying about "wasting one's vote." This is done by voting for the favorite *and* the candidate considered most acceptable who seems to have a serious chance of winning. This way a voter is able to express a sincere preference and at the same time vote for the candidate who would be preferable if the favorite cannot win.

Apart from the question of wasting one's vote, plurality voting is fundamentally unfair to a voter who may have a hard time deciding who is the best candidate in a crowded field but can choose the two or more candidates considered most acceptable. Approval voting thus provides more flexible options and thereby encourages a truer expression of preferences than does plurality voting.

2. *It elects the strongest candidate.* It is entirely possible in a three-candidate plurality race in which A wins 25 percent of the vote, B 35 percent, and C 40 percent that the loser, A, is the strongest candidate who would beat B in a separate two-way contest (because C supporters would vote for A), and would beat C in a separate two-way contest (because B supporters would vote for A). Even a runoff election between the top vote getters (B and C) would not show up this fact. On the other hand, approval voting in all likelihood would reveal A to be the strongest candidate because some B and C supporters—who liked A as much or almost as much—would cast second approval votes for A, who would thereby become the winner.

It is not hard to think of actual elections in which minority candidates triumphed with less than 50 percent of the vote who almost surely would have lost if they had been in contests with just one of their opponents. For example, a liberal, John Lindsay, won the 1969 mayoral election in New York City against two opponents who split the moderate-conservative vote (58 percent of the total); and a conservative, James Buckley, won the 1970 U.S. Senate election in New York against two opponents who split the moderate-liberal vote (61 percent of the total). This problem of a minority candidate's eking out a victory in a crowded field is aggravated the more candidates there are in a race. Moreover, as the examples indicate, the minority-candidate bias of plurality voting is not ideological: it can afflict both liberals and conservatives. Approval voting, by contrast, is biased in favor of the strongest candidate, especially a candidate like A in the earlier example who would defeat each of the others in head-to-head contests.

3. *It is best for the parties.* For reasons just given, approval voting would tend to favor the strongest and most viable candidates in each party. It is unlikely, for example, that Barry Goldwater would have won the Republican presidential nomination in 1964, or George McGovern the Democratic presidential nomination in 1972, if there had been approval voting in the state presidential primaries. Both nominees were probably minority candidates even within their own parties, and both lost decisively in the general election.

4. *It gives minority candidates their proper due.* In 1968, George Wallace dropped from 21 percent support in the polls in September to 14 percent in the actual vote on election day in November. It seems likely that the one-third of Wallace supporters who deserted him in favor of one of the major-party candidates did so because they thought he had no serious chance of winning—the wasted vote phenomenon. But, if there had been approval voting, Wallace would almost surely have retained his original supporters, some of whom would also have voted for Nixon or Humphrey. One of these candidates would have won, probably with more than 50 percent of the vote (Nixon received 43.4 percent in the election; Humphrey, 42.7 percent), but Wallace would have registered much more substantial support than he did. With approval voting, minority candidates would get their proper due, but majority candidates would generally win.

5. *It is insensitive to the number of candidates running.* Because ballots may be cast for as many candidates as the voter wishes under approval voting, if new candidates enter it is still possible to vote for one or more of them without being forced to withdraw support from old candidates. Plurality voting, on the other hand, is very sensitive to the number of candidates running. As the number of contenders increases, the plurality contest becomes more and more one of who can inch out whom in a crowded field rather than who is the strongest and most acceptable candidate.

Thus, when Jimmy Carter won less than 30 percent of the vote in the New Hampshire Democratic primary in 1976, the significance of his victory could be questioned. This gave the media an opportunity to pass judgment, which they gleefully did. Approval voting, by contrast, by better revealing the overall acceptability of the candidates independent of the field in which they run, more accurately mirrors each candidate's true level of support and gives more meaning to the voter's judgment. A side benefit would be that the voters, not the media, would weigh in more heavily in the selection process.

As an example of a recent election in which the overall acceptability of candidates was difficult to ascertain, consider the Democratic primary in the 1977 New York City mayoral election. With no candidate receiving as much as 20 percent of the vote, and six candidates receiving more than 10 percent, a judgment about who the most popular candidate was seems highly dubious. Even the runoff election that pitted Edward Koch (19.8 percent of the plurality vote) against Mario Cuomo (18.6 percent of the plurality vote) said nothing about how the winner, Koch, would have fared in runoffs against the other four candidates who received between 11.0 and 18.0 percent of the plurality vote. Although Koch may have been the candidate more acceptable to the voters than any other candidate in this election, plurality voting, even with a runoff, did not demonstrate this to be the case.

An Example. The following hypothetical example perhaps best dramatizes the different effects of plurality voting and approval voting:

	Plurality Voting	*Approval Voting*
Candidate X	25%	30%
Candidate Y	24%	51%

In this example, which assumes X and Y are the top two candidates in the race and several other candidates split the remaining vote, X just wins under plurality voting. Yet X is approved of by less than one-third of the voters, whereas Y is acceptable to more than one-half of the voters.

Is it fair that X, unacceptable to 70 percent of the electorate, should be considered the "winner" simply because he is the first choice of more voters than any other candidate in a crowded field? He may be liked by the biggest minority of voters (25 percent), but in my opinion the voting system should also register the fact that he is disliked—that is, not approved of—by all but 30 percent of the voters.

Approval voting would show up the fact that Y is acceptable to many more voters than X. Of course, the plurality voting winner and the approval voting winner will often be the same, and then there will be no problem. However, the discrepancy between plurality and approval voting winners seems not so infrequent, even in races with as few as three candidates, to be dismissed as a rare event.

6. *It could increase voter turnout.* By giving voters more flexible options, approval voting could encourage greater voter turnout, although this is difficult to establish until we have some experience with approval voting. It seems likely, however, that some voters do not go to the polls because they cannot make up their minds about who is the single best candidate in a multi-candidate race. By giving such voters the option to vote for two or more candidates if they have no clear favorite, they probably would have more incentive to vote in the first place.

7. *It is superior to preferential voting.* An election reform that has been tried in a few places in the United States (for example, Ann Arbor, Michigan) shares many of the advantages of approval voting. It is called preferential voting and it requires each voter to rank the candidates from best to worst. If no candidate receives a majority of first-place votes, the candidate with the fewest first-place votes is dropped and the second-place votes of his supporters are given to the remaining candidates. The elimination process continues, with lower-place votes of the voters whose preferred candidates are eliminated being transferred to the candidates that survive, until one candidate receives a majority of votes.

Apart from the practical problems of implementing a ranking system, preferential voting has a major drawback: it may eliminate the candidate acceptable to the most voters. In the hypothetical example given in argument 2 above, A would have been eliminated at the outset. Yet, A would have defeated B and C in separate two-way contests, and was, therefore, the strongest candidate and probably would have won with approval voting.

A less serious drawback of preferential voting is that the candidate with the most first-place votes may be displaced after the transfers have been made to determine the majority winner. This may greatly upset that candidate's supporters, particularly if they are a large minority, and lead to questions about the legitimacy of the system. This challenge cannot be mounted against approval voting since approval votes are indistinguishable—whether these votes are first-place, second-place, or whatever is not recorded, so no portion of the winner's total can be judged "inferior."

8. *Practicalities*. It may be thought that, even given the virtues of approval voting, it would make little difference in a real election. This is so because the candidates would encourage voters to vote just for themselves (bullet voting) to keep down the vote totals of their opponents. Yet, even if the candidates made such an appeal, it would probably not be effective, particularly in a crowded race in which voters had difficulty distinguishing their single favorite. As evidence to support this assertion, in an approval voting experiment involving several hundred Pennsylvania voters prior to their 1976 primaries, 72 percent of the voters voted for two or more of the eight candidates listed on their sample ballots.

How can approval voting be implemented? There are a multitude of laws governing the conduct of elections, but consider the statute in New Hampshire for voting in the presidential primaries. To enact approval voting in these elections would require only the substitution of the words in parentheses for the preceding words:

> Every qualified voter . . . shall have opportunity . . . to vote his preference (preferences), on the ballot of his party, for his choice (choices) for one person (any persons) to be the candidate (candidates) of his political party for president of the United States and one person (any persons) to be the candidate (candidates) of his political party for vice president of the United States.

I have been assured by voting machine manufacturers that their equipment could be easily adjusted to allow for approval voting. In jurisdictions which use paper ballots, allowing voters to mark their ballots for more than one candidate will make vote counting somewhat more tedious and time consuming, but this should not be a major barrier to the adoption of approval voting.

I am completely convinced that approval voting will be the election reform of the 20th century, just as the Australian, or secret, ballot printed by the government with the names of all authorized candidates was the election reform of the 19th century. In effect, the principle of "one man, one vote" in plurality voting becomes the principle of "one candidate, one vote" with approval voting.

Proposal for a Regional Primary System

National Association of Secretaries of State

Approved February 12, 1999
Model Presidential Primary Legislation

SECTION 1

Findings and Declaration

1. The people of the state of _____ acting through their elected legislative representation find and declare that:
   a. The quadrennial election of the President and Vice President of the United States is among the most important civic acts of the voters of the state of _____.
   b. The Process leading to nomination of candidates for President and Vice President of the United States should be as open and participatory as possible.
   c. It will enhance voter participation, strengthen the political process and protect the rights of all states and their citizens to have a coordinated, orderly and defined electoral schedule.
   d. The State of _____ will participate in a rotating regional presidential primary system as defined herein.
   e. Understanding the historically important role that smaller states have played in the presidential selection process in terms of "retail politics," the states of New Hampshire and Iowa shall be allowed to conduct their primary election or caucus prior to the commencement of the rotation schedule.

129

SECTION 2

Definition

"Presidential Primary" is the official primary election conducted or sanctioned by the state of _____ held in any year that is evenly divisible by the number four at which delegations to national party conventions are to be chosen.

SECTION 3

Notwithstanding any other provision of law to the contrary, the state of _____, consistent with its decision to affiliate with Region _____, as defined by the National Association of Secretaries of State, shall hold its presidential primary not sooner than the first Tuesday after the first Monday in March, April, May and June 2004, but in no case later than six (6) days after said Monday in the order defined in Section 4; and shall rotate in subsequent presidential election years as specified in Section 5.

SECTION 4

For the purposes of presidential primaries the following states should be grouped as follows:

Eastern Region (1)

Connecticut, Delaware, Maine, Maryland, Massachusetts, New Jersey, New York, Pennsylvania, Rhode Island, Vermont, West Virginia and the District of Columbia.

Southern Region (2)

Alabama, Arkansas, Florida, Georgia, Kentucky, Louisiana, Mississippi, North Carolina, Oklahoma, South Carolina, Tennessee, Texas, Virginia, Puerto Rico and the Virgin Islands.

Midwestern Region (3)

Illinois, Indiana, Kansas, Michigan, Minnesota, Missouri, Nebraska, North Dakota, Ohio, South Dakota and Wisconsin.

Western Region (4)

Alaska, Arizona, California, Colorado, Hawaii, Idaho, Montana, Nevada, New Mexico, Oregon, Utah, Washington, Wyoming and Guam.

It is the intent that Region 1 begin in March 2004 with other regions in numerical sequence in April, May and June 2004. In subsequent cycles, the first region to hold its primary would move to last and all others in sequence shall move up.

SECTION 5

Rotation of the Date of the Presidential Primary

In the presidential primary elections subsequent to the year 2004, the date of the election shall be the first Tuesday of the month preceding the month of the most recent presidential primary election, except that if the most recent presidential primary election was conducted on the first Tuesday of March the date of the election shall be the first Tuesday of June.

Index

affirmative action, 11–12, 14–15, 19, 86, 88, 89, 90–92, 120
Aldrich, John, 35–36
apportionment of delegates, 87, 90, 96–97
approval voting, 117, 123–27

Bennett, William, 60
Berdahl, Clarence, 106
Biden, Joseph, 66
Blunt, Roy, 66–67
Bond, John, 73
bonus delegates, 20–21
Bradley, Bill, 59, 66
Brams, Stephen J., 123–27
Broder, David, 29, 51, 61–62, 71
Bryce, Alfred, 65
Buchanan, Pat, 40, 62–63
bullet voting, 127
Bush, George H. W., 68(table), 70
Bush, George W., 65, 66–67

campaign finance reform (1974), 16–17
campaign financing, 16–17, 43, 52, 57
candidate preferences, of delegates: binding, 5, 18–19, 20, 28, 46, 63–64, 104, 109, 116, 117; opportunity for, 10, 63, 98; among party leadership, 41, 64–67; by proportional rule, 15, 17, 19–20, 21, 34–35, 109; reflecting state preferences, 15, 18, 66; requirement to disclose, 15–16, 116; and second

choice options, 40–41; support threshold for, 20, 21, 34–35, 117; under traditional mixed system, 37–39, 45–46, 47; uncommitted, 10, 19, 34, 63, 65, 66, 98, 104, 116; and unit rule, 10, 90, 95–96. *See also* approval voting; caucus-convention; delegate selection; primaries
Carlton, Warren, 63
Carter, Jimmy, 17, 18, 19, 20, 68, 71, 73; and primary selection, 30, 33, 39, 40–41, 67
caucus, congressional, 3–4
caucus-convention, 5, 8, 27, 42; ideology in, 54–55; in national pre-primary convention proposal, 116, 117–18; and party affiliation, 18, 97–98; proxies in, 9–10, 86, 90, 94; public notice of, 9, 86, 90, 97–98; public participation in, 52–53, 54–55; quorum requirements in, 10, 86, 90, 95; and reforms, 10, 13, 15, 18
Ceaser, James W., 31
Cheney, Richard, 60–61
Clinton, Bill, 33, 68(table), 70–71
coalition building, 31, 35–36
Col, Dan, 32
Commager, Henry Steele, 68
Cranston, Alan, 115
Cronin, Thomas, 113–21

Dahl, Robert, 51
Daley, Richard, 14

133

About the Authors

Robert E. DiClerico is Eberly Professor of Political Science at West Virginia University and author of *The American President; Few Are Chosen: Problems in Presidential Selection; Analyzing the Presidency;* and *Political Parties, Campaigns, and Elections.*

James W. Davis is emeritus professor of political science, Western Washington University, and author of *Presidential Primaries: Road to the White House; National Conventions in an Age of Party Reform; U.S. Presidential Primaries and the Caucus-Convention System;* and *The American Presidency: A New Perspective.*